Chapter 1: Introduction to Puppetry...11
    History of Puppetry...11
    Importance of Character Creation..12
    Overview of Puppet Types..12

Chapter 2: Understanding Your Audience...14
    Identifying Target Audience...14
    Tailoring Characters...15
    Engaging Different Age Groups..16

Chapter 3: The Basics of Character Design..17
    Elements of Character Design...17
    Visual Appeal..18
    Emotional Connection..18

Chapter 4: Types of Puppets...20
    Hand Puppets..20
        History and Evolution..20
        Design and Construction..21
        Performance Techniques..21
    Marionettes...22
        Historical Context..22
        Construction and Design...22
        Manipulation Techniques...23
    Shadow Puppets..23
        Origins and Cultural Significance...23
        Design and Creation..23
        Performance Techniques..24

Chapter 5: Developing a Character Concept..25
    Brainstorming Ideas..25
    Character Backstory..26
    Defining Character Goals...26

Chapter 6: Personality Traits and Archetypes..28
    Common Archetypes..28
    Creating Unique Personalities...29

Balancing Traits..30
Chapter 7: Physical Attributes of Puppets..32
Size and Shape..32
Color Schemes..33
Material Choices..34
Chapter 8: Voice and Speech Patterns..35
Creating Distinct Voices..35
    1. Character Background...35
    2. Emotional Range..35
    3. Vocal Techniques...36
Speech Techniques..36
    1. Pacing and Rhythm..36
    2. Articulation and Clarity...37
    3. Emotional Inflection..37
Using Accents..37
    1. Research and Authenticity...38
    2. Practice and Refinement...38
    3. Integrating Accents into Character Development..................38
Table of Vocal Techniques..39
Chapter 9: Movement and Expression..40
Body Language..40
    Gesture and Movement..41
    Spatial Awareness...41
Facial Expressions..41
    Creating Emotional Resonance..42
    Facial Manipulation Techniques..42
Movement Techniques...43
    Timing and Rhythm...43
    Choreography and Blocking..43
    Improvisation in Movement..44
Chapter 10: Crafting a Puppet's Backstory...45
Importance of Backstory..45
Integrating History..46
Motivations and Conflicts..47
Chapter 11: The Role of Humor in Puppetry..49

- Types of Humor 49
- Timing and Delivery 50
  - 1. Pacing 50
  - 2. Physical Timing 50
  - 3. Vocal Delivery 51
  - 4. Audience Interaction 51
- Creating Comedic Characters 51
  - 1. Defining Character Traits 51
  - 2. Relationships and Dynamics 52
  - 3. Visual Design 52
  - 4. Backstory and Motivation 52
  - 5. Experimentation and Adaptation 52

Chapter 12: Emotional Depth in Characters 53
- Building Empathy 53
- Emotional Arcs 54
- Relatable Struggles 55

Chapter 13: Cultural Influences on Character Creation 58
- Cultural Sensitivity 58
- Incorporating Traditions 59
- Diverse Characters 60

Chapter 14: Collaborating with Other Artists 61
- Working with Writers, Designers, and Performers 61

Chapter 15: The Importance of Rehearsal 64
- Practicing Characterization 64
- Timing and Rhythm 65
- Feedback Loops 66

Chapter 16: Creating Dynamic Relationships 68
- Character Interactions 68
  - Establishing Relationships 68
  - Dialogue and Communication Styles 69
  - Physical Interactions 69
- Conflict and Resolution 70
  - Types of Conflict 70
  - Building Tension 71
  - Resolution and Growth 71

- Group Dynamics...72
  - Character Roles within Groups...72
  - Group Interactions..73
  - Impact of Group Dynamics on Character Development................................73
- Chapter 17: The Role of Music and Sound..75
  - Choosing Soundscapes..75
  - Musical Themes...76
  - Enhancing Character Presence...77
- Chapter 18: Designing Costumes for Puppets..79
  - Costume Basics...79
    - 1. Character Identity..79
    - 2. Functionality..79
    - 3. Visual Impact...80
    - 4. Cultural Context..80
    - 5. Layering and Texture..80
  - Fabric Choices...80
    - 1. Types of Fabrics..80
    - 2. Color Theory...81
    - 3. Patterns and Prints...82
  - Accessorizing Characters..82
    - 1. Types of Accessories..82
    - 2. Personalization..83
    - 3. Balance and Proportion...83
    - 4. Practical Considerations..83
- Chapter 19: Building a Puppet from Scratch..84
  - Materials Needed..84
    - 1. Base Structure..84
    - 2. Fabric and Textiles...84
    - 3. Adhesives and Fasteners...85
    - 4. Features and Accessories..85
    - 5. Tools...85
  - Step-by-Step Guide...86
    - Step 1: Conceptualize Your Puppet...86
    - Step 2: Create the Base Structure...86
    - Step 3: Add Features...87

- Step 4: Dress Your Puppet ... 87
- Step 5: Assemble the Puppet ... 87
- Step 6: Test Movement and Expression ... 87
- Step 7: Final Touches ... 87
- Tips for Beginners ... 88
  - 1. Start Simple ... 88
  - 2. Experiment with Materials ... 88
  - 3. Embrace Mistakes ... 88
  - 4. Seek Inspiration ... 88
  - 5. Join a Community ... 89
  - 6. Practice Regularly ... 89
  - 7. Have Fun! ... 89

Chapter 20: Using Technology in Puppetry ... 90
- Digital Puppetry ... 90
- Animation Techniques ... 91
- Interactive Elements ... 92

Chapter 21: The Ethics of Puppetry ... 94
- Respecting Cultures ... 94
- Avoiding Stereotypes ... 95
- Responsible Storytelling ... 95

Chapter 22: Creating a Puppet Show Script ... 97
- Structure of a Script ... 97
- Dialogue Writing ... 98
  - Character Voice ... 98
  - Subtext ... 98
  - Rhythm and Pacing ... 99
- Scene Development ... 99
  - Setting the Scene ... 99
  - Action and Movement ... 99
  - Character Interaction ... 100

Chapter 23: The Role of Lighting in Puppetry ... 101
- Setting the Mood ... 101
- Highlighting Characters ... 102
- Practical Techniques ... 103

Chapter 24: Marketing Your Puppet Characters ... 105

- Branding 105
  - Defining Your Brand Identity 105
  - Creating a Visual Identity 106
  - Consistency Across Platforms 106
- Social Media Strategies 106
  - Choosing the Right Platforms 106
  - Content Creation 107
  - Engagement and Community Building 107
- Building an Audience 107
  - Networking with Other Artists 108
  - Participating in Events 108
  - Utilizing Email Marketing 108
  - Offering Merchandise 108
  - Tracking and Analyzing Your Efforts 108

Chapter 25: The Impact of Puppetry on Education 110
- Educational Benefits 110
- Creating Learning Characters 110
- Engaging Students 111

Chapter 26: Puppetry in Therapy 114
- Therapeutic Benefits 114
- Creating Healing Characters 114
- Case Studies 115

Chapter 27: Exploring Different Genres 117
- Fantasy 117
- Comedy 117
- Drama 118
- And More 119

Chapter 28: The Evolution of Puppetry 122
- Historical Changes 122
  - Table 1: Key Historical Milestones in Puppetry 123
- Modern Innovations 123
  - Table 2: Modern Innovations in Puppetry 124
- Future Trends 124
  - Table 3: Future Trends in Puppetry 125

Chapter 29: Creating Memorable Side Characters 126

- Supporting Roles 126
- Enhancing Main Characters 126
- Adding Depth 127

Chapter 30: The Art of Improvisation 130
- Spontaneity in Performance 130
- Character Flexibility 130
- Audience Interaction 131

Chapter 31: Puppetry in Film and Television 134
- Adapting Characters 134
- Behind-the-Scenes 134
- Iconic Puppet Characters 135

Chapter 32: The Role of Puppetry in Storytelling 137
- Narrative Techniques 137
  - 1. Visual Storytelling 137
  - 2. Dialogue and Voice 137
  - 3. Symbolism and Metaphor 138
- Character Arcs 138
  - 1. The Hero's Journey 139
  - 2. Transformation and Growth 139
  - 3. Relatable Flaws 139
- Thematic Elements 140
  - 1. Social Commentary 140
  - 2. The Power of Imagination 140
  - 3. The Human Experience 141

Chapter 33: Building a Puppet Character Portfolio 142
- Documenting Characters 142
  - Character Profiles 142
  - Visual Documentation 143
  - Performance Notes 144
- Showcasing Skills 144
  - Highlighting Craftsmanship 144
  - Performance Highlights 145
  - Workshops and Teaching 145
- Professional Presentation 145
  - Portfolio Format 146

- Branding and Identity...........146
- Regular Updates...........146

Chapter 34: The Psychology of Character Creation...........148
- Understanding Audience Perception...........148
- Character Relatability...........148
- Psychological Depth...........149

Chapter 35: Engaging with the Puppetry Community...........151
- Networking...........151
- Collaborations...........151
- Learning Opportunities...........152

Chapter 36: The Business of Puppetry...........154
- Monetizing Your Skills...........154
- Funding Projects...........154
- Managing Finances...........154

Chapter 37: Adapting Characters for Different Mediums...........157
- Stage, Screen, and Digital Platforms...........157
- Understanding the Medium...........157
- Character Design Considerations...........158
- Performance Techniques...........158
- Storytelling Across Mediums...........159
- Collaborative Creation...........159
- Conclusion...........160

Chapter 38: The Role of Puppetry in Activism...........161
- Creating Awareness...........161
- Engaging Audiences...........161
- Powerful Messages...........162

Chapter 39: Character Development Workshops...........164
- Facilitating Workshops...........164
- Exercises and Activities...........164
  - 1. Character Brainstorming Sessions...........165
  - 2. Character Sketching...........165
  - 3. Voice and Movement Exploration...........165
  - 4. Backstory Development...........165
  - 5. Group Feedback Sessions...........166
- Building Skills...........166

- 1. Creative Thinking..166
- 2. Communication Skills..166
- 3. Problem-Solving Abilities...166
- 4. Empathy and Understanding...167
- 5. Technical Skills..167

Chapter 40: The Influence of Literature on Puppetry..........................168
- Classic Literature...168
  - The Timeless Appeal of Shakespeare..168
  - Fairy Tales and Folklore...168
  - Mythology and Epic Tales...168
- Modern Adaptations...169
  - Young Adult Literature..169
  - Graphic Novels and Comics..169
  - Literary Classics Reimagined..170
- Character Inspirations..170
  - Archetypes and Their Adaptations..170
  - Complex Characters and Emotional Depth..171
  - Iconic Literary Figures..171

Chapter 41: The Importance of Feedback..172
- Receiving Critiques...172
- Iterating on Characters..172
- Growth Mindset...173

Chapter 42: Creating a Puppet Character for Social Change..............175
- Identifying Issues..175
- Character Messaging..175
- Impactful Storytelling...175
  - Case Study: The Eco-Warrior Puppet..177
  - Case Study: The Mental Health Advocate..177
  - Case Study: The Social Justice Puppet..177

Chapter 43: The Intersection of Puppetry and Visual Arts.................179
- Artistic Techniques...179
- Collaborating with Visual Artists...180
- Mixed Media...180

Chapter 44: The Role of Puppetry in Cultural Preservation................183
- Traditional Puppetry Forms..183

    Storytelling Heritage..183

    Reviving Lost Arts...184

Chapter 45: Exploring Puppetry Techniques from Around the World........187

    Global Styles..187

        Asian Puppetry..187

        European Puppetry...187

        African Puppetry..188

    Unique Techniques..188

        Manipulation Styles..188

        Material and Craftsmanship..188

        Performance Techniques..189

    Cultural Significance...189

        Preservation of Traditions...190

        Community Engagement..190

        Global Exchange..190

Chapter 46: The Future of Puppetry..192

    Emerging Trends...192

    Innovations in Character Creation..192

    Predictions..192

Chapter 47: Building a Puppet Character for Children....................................195

    Child-Friendly Design...195

    Educational Elements..195

    Engaging Narratives..196

Chapter 48: The Role of Puppetry in Festivals and Events..............................198

    Creating Event Characters..198

        1. Theme Alignment..198

        2. Cultural Representation...198

        3. Visual Appeal..198

        4. Interactive Elements...198

    Engaging Audiences...199

        1. Storytelling Techniques..199

        2. Use of Humor...199

        3. Dynamic Performances...199

        4. Audience Participation...200

        5. Social Media Engagement..200

Performance Tips..200
    1. Rehearsal and Preparation..200
    2. Adaptability...200
    3. Safety Considerations..201
    4. Feedback and Reflection..201
    5. Networking Opportunities...201
    6. Enjoy the Moment..201

Chapter 49: The Influence of Technology on Character Creation..........203
Digital Tools..203
    Case Study: The Digital Puppet Revolution...........................204
Animation Software..204
    Case Study: Animated Puppetry in Education.....................205
Virtual Puppetry...205
    Case Study: Virtual Reality Puppet Theatre..........................206

Chapter 50: The Art of Character Transformation................................207
Character Growth..207
Physical Changes..207
Narrative Evolution...208

Chapter 51: Celebrating Iconic Puppet Characters..............................211
Case Studies..211
    The Muppets..211
    Sesame Street...211
    Pinocchio..211
    Spitting Image..212
Impact on Culture...212
    Representation and Diversity..212
    Social Commentary..213
    Emotional Connection...213
Lessons Learned..213
    The Power of Storytelling...213
    Embracing Diversity...214
    Humor as a Tool for Connection..214
    The Importance of Collaboration...214

Chapter 1: Introduction to Puppetry

History of Puppetry

Puppetry, an art form that transcends cultures and epochs, has a rich and varied history that dates back thousands of years. The earliest recorded instances of puppetry can be traced to ancient civilizations, where figures crafted from wood, cloth, and other materials were manipulated to tell stories, convey moral lessons, and entertain audiences. In ancient Egypt, for example, puppets were used in religious ceremonies, while in Greece, they played a role in theatrical performances, often serving as a bridge between the divine and the mortal. The art of puppetry flourished during the Middle Ages, particularly in Europe, where marionettes and shadow puppets became popular forms of entertainment. Traveling troupes would perform in town squares, captivating audiences with their intricate storytelling and lively characters. The Italian commedia dell'arte, a form of improvisational theater, heavily influenced the development of puppetry, introducing iconic characters such as Harlequin and Pierrot, whose exaggerated traits and comedic antics continue to inspire puppeteers today. As we journey through the ages, we find that puppetry has not only entertained but also served as a powerful medium for social commentary. In the 18th and 19th centuries, puppetry became a vehicle for political satire, with puppeteers using their craft to critique societal norms and challenge authority. The art form adapted to the changing times, reflecting the values and concerns of each era. In the 20th century, puppetry experienced a renaissance, with the advent of television and film introducing new possibilities for the medium. Iconic figures such as Jim Henson's Muppets brought puppetry into the mainstream, captivating audiences of all ages with their charm, humor, and relatability. Today, puppetry continues to evolve, embracing modern technology and innovative techniques while remaining rooted in its rich historical traditions. The history of puppetry is not merely a chronicle of its evolution; it is a testament to the enduring power of storytelling and the human desire to connect through art. As we delve into the world of puppetry, we uncover the threads that bind us to our past and the potential for creativity that lies ahead.

Importance of Character Creation

At the heart of puppetry lies the art of character creation, a process that transforms inanimate objects into vibrant, relatable beings. The significance of character creation cannot be overstated; it is the foundation upon which compelling narratives are built. A well-crafted character breathes life into a puppet, allowing it to resonate with audiences on an emotional level. Character creation in puppetry is a multifaceted endeavor, encompassing a range of elements that contribute to the puppet's identity. From personality traits and physical attributes to voice and movement, each aspect plays a crucial role in shaping how the character is perceived. A puppet's character must be carefully considered, as it influences not only the story being told but also the audience's engagement and connection to the performance. Moreover, the process of character creation encourages creativity and imagination. Puppeteers are tasked with envisioning the world their characters inhabit, exploring their motivations, desires, and conflicts. This exploration fosters a deeper understanding of the human experience, as puppeteers draw from their own lives and observations to create characters that reflect the complexities of existence. In addition to fostering creativity, character creation serves as a means of communication. Puppets often embody themes and ideas that resonate with audiences, allowing for the exploration of social issues, cultural narratives, and personal experiences. Through the lens of puppetry, complex topics can be addressed in a manner that is accessible and engaging, inviting dialogue and reflection. Furthermore, the importance of character creation extends beyond the individual puppet. A well-developed character can enhance the dynamics of a puppet ensemble, contributing to the overall narrative and enriching the audience's experience. The interplay between characters, their relationships, and their interactions creates a tapestry of storytelling that captivates and entertains. In essence, character creation is the lifeblood of puppetry. It is the process through which puppets transcend their physical form, becoming vessels for storytelling and emotional expression. As we embark on this journey into the art of puppetry, we will explore the intricacies of character creation, uncovering the techniques and insights that will empower you to bring your own puppet characters to life.

Overview of Puppet Types

Puppetry is a diverse art form, encompassing a wide array of puppet types, each with its own unique characteristics and methods of manipulation. Understanding the various types of puppets is essential for any aspiring puppeteer, as it informs the choices made during character creation and performance. One of the most recognizable forms of puppetry is the marionette, a puppet controlled by strings or wires. Marionettes are often intricately designed, featuring articulated limbs that allow for a range of expressive movements. The skill required to manipulate marionettes effectively is considerable, as the puppeteer must master the delicate balance between control and fluidity. The elegance of marionette performances often evokes a sense of wonder, as these puppets dance and interact with one another in a captivating display of artistry. Another popular type of puppet is the hand puppet, which is operated by the puppeteer's hand inserted into the puppet's body. Hand puppets are known for their immediacy and intimacy, allowing for direct interaction between the puppeteer and the audience. This form of puppetry is particularly effective in engaging young viewers, as the puppets can convey emotions and expressions through simple gestures and vocalizations. The versatility of hand puppets makes them a staple in children's theater and educational settings. Shadow puppetry, a form that dates back centuries, utilizes flat, cut-out figures that are projected onto a screen using light. This technique creates a mesmerizing visual experience, as the interplay of light and shadow brings the characters to life. Shadow puppetry has a rich cultural heritage, with distinct styles emerging from various regions around the world. The simplicity of shadow puppetry allows for imaginative storytelling, as the audience's imagination fills in the details of the narrative. In contrast, rod puppets are manipulated using rods attached to their limbs, allowing for a different style of movement. This type of puppet is often used in traditional folk performances and can range from simple designs to elaborate creations. The use of rods provides a unique opportunity for puppeteers to explore dynamic movements and interactions between characters, adding depth to the storytelling. Finally, we have the emerging realm of digital puppetry, where technology and animation converge to create new possibilities for character creation and performance. Digital puppetry utilizes software and hardware to manipulate virtual characters in real-time, allowing for innovative storytelling techniques that push the boundaries of traditional puppetry. This form of puppetry is gaining traction in various media, including film, video games, and online platforms, offering exciting opportunities for creative expression. Each type of puppet brings its own set of challenges and rewards, influencing the way characters are developed and stories are told. As we delve deeper into the art of puppetry, we will explore the nuances of each puppet type, examining how they can be harnessed to create compelling characters that resonate with audiences.

Chapter 2: Understanding Your Audience

The art of puppetry is not merely about the puppets themselves; it is an intricate dance between the puppeteer and the audience. Understanding your audience is paramount to creating characters that resonate, evoke emotions, and leave a lasting impression. This chapter delves into the nuances of audience engagement, exploring how to identify your target demographic, tailor your characters accordingly, and engage different age groups effectively.

Identifying Target Audience

To embark on the journey of character creation, one must first understand who will be receiving the performance. Identifying your target audience is akin to setting the stage for a grand production; it shapes the narrative, influences character design, and determines the overall tone of the performance. The first step in this process is to conduct thorough research. This involves analyzing demographic data, understanding cultural backgrounds, and recognizing the interests and preferences of potential viewers. Are they children, adults, or a mixed audience? Each group brings its own set of expectations and emotional responses, which must be considered when crafting your characters. For instance, a puppet show aimed at children may require vibrant colors, exaggerated features, and whimsical personalities. Characters in this realm often embody innocence and curiosity, serving as guides through fantastical adventures. In contrast, a performance designed for adults may delve into more complex themes, exploring the intricacies of human relationships or societal issues. Here, characters may possess depth, nuance, and a touch of irony, inviting the audience to reflect on their own experiences. Moreover, understanding the cultural context of your audience is essential. Different cultures have unique storytelling traditions, values, and humor. A character that resonates in one culture may fall flat in another. Engaging with local communities, attending cultural events, and immersing oneself in the traditions of the audience can provide invaluable insights that inform character creation. Additionally, consider the emotional landscape of your audience. What are their hopes, fears, and aspirations? Characters that reflect these emotions can create a powerful connection, allowing the audience to see themselves within the narrative. This connection fosters empathy and understanding, transforming a simple puppet show into a shared experience that transcends the stage. In summary, identifying your target audience is a multifaceted process that requires careful consideration and research. By understanding who your audience is, you can create characters that resonate deeply, ensuring that your puppetry not only entertains but also enriches the lives of those who experience it.

Tailoring Characters

Once you have a clear understanding of your audience, the next step is to tailor your characters to meet their expectations and desires. This process involves a delicate balance of creativity and strategy, as you seek to create characters that are both engaging and relatable. Begin by defining the core attributes of your characters. What are their motivations, desires, and conflicts? These elements should align with the interests of your audience. For example, if your target demographic is children, consider creating characters that embody qualities such as bravery, kindness, and curiosity. These traits not only resonate with young viewers but also serve as valuable lessons that can inspire and educate. Conversely, if your audience consists of adults, you may wish to explore more complex character traits. Characters that grapple with moral dilemmas, face personal challenges, or navigate intricate relationships can captivate adult audiences. By presenting characters that reflect the complexities of real life, you invite viewers to engage in deeper conversations and reflections. Moreover, consider the visual aspects of your characters. The design of a puppet can significantly impact how it is perceived by the audience. Bright colors and playful shapes may appeal to children, while more subdued tones and intricate details may resonate with adults. The physical attributes of your puppets should align with the emotional tone of the narrative, enhancing the overall experience. Another crucial aspect of tailoring characters is to ensure that they possess a unique voice. The way a character speaks, their choice of words, and their speech patterns can convey a wealth of information about their personality. For instance, a character who speaks in rhymes or uses playful language may be more appealing to children, while a character with a sophisticated vocabulary may resonate with an adult audience. Furthermore, consider the relationships between characters. The dynamics of these relationships can provide insight into the characters themselves and create opportunities for humor, conflict, and growth. By crafting interactions that reflect the audience's experiences, you can create a sense of familiarity and connection that enhances the overall narrative. In essence, tailoring characters is an art form that requires a deep understanding of your audience's preferences, emotions, and cultural context. By aligning your characters with these elements, you can create a captivating experience that resonates on multiple levels, leaving a lasting impact on your viewers.

Engaging Different Age Groups

Engaging different age groups presents a unique set of challenges and opportunities for puppeteers. Each age group has distinct preferences, cognitive abilities, and emotional responses, which must be considered when creating characters and narratives. For young children, engagement often hinges on visual stimulation and simplicity. Characters that are colorful, animated, and larger-than-life can capture their attention and spark their imagination. Incorporating elements of playfulness, such as silly voices, exaggerated movements, and interactive storytelling, can further enhance their engagement. Children thrive on repetition and familiarity, so characters that appear consistently throughout a performance can create a sense of comfort and anticipation. In addition, humor plays a vital role in engaging young audiences. Simple jokes, physical comedy, and playful antics can elicit laughter and joy, making the experience memorable. Characters that embody childlike wonder and curiosity can serve as relatable figures, guiding young viewers through the narrative while encouraging them to explore their own imaginations. As children grow into pre-teens and teenagers, their engagement shifts. They begin to seek more complex narratives and characters that reflect their own experiences and struggles. At this stage, characters should embody traits that resonate with their evolving identities, such as independence, self-discovery, and friendship. Incorporating themes of resilience, social issues, and personal growth can foster a deeper connection with this age group. Moreover, the use of technology can enhance engagement for older audiences. Integrating multimedia elements, such as projections, soundscapes, or interactive components, can create a dynamic experience that captivates their attention. Characters that embrace contemporary themes or reflect current societal issues can also resonate with teenagers, encouraging them to engage in meaningful discussions. For adult audiences, engagement often revolves around depth and complexity. Characters that grapple with existential questions, moral dilemmas, or societal challenges can provoke thought and reflection. The use of subtlety, irony, and nuanced storytelling can create a rich tapestry of emotions that resonates with adult viewers. Additionally, the incorporation of humor can take on a different form for adults. Wit, satire, and clever wordplay can engage this demographic, inviting them to reflect on their own experiences while enjoying the performance. Characters that embody relatable struggles, such as career challenges or relationship dynamics, can create a sense of camaraderie and understanding among adult audiences.

Chapter 3: The Basics of Character Design

 Elements of Character Design

Character design is a multifaceted art form that combines creativity, psychology, and a deep understanding of the medium in which the character will exist. At its core, character design is about creating a visual representation that resonates with the audience while conveying the essence of the character's personality, background, and role in the narrative. The first element of character design is shape. Shapes can evoke different feelings and associations. For instance, round shapes often convey friendliness and approachability, while sharp angles can suggest danger or aggression. When designing a puppet character, consider the shapes that best represent the character's traits. A whimsical, jovial character might be designed with soft, rounded features, while a villainous character could be depicted with angular, jagged lines. Color is another vital element in character design. Colors can evoke emotions and set the tone for a character's personality. Bright, vibrant colors may suggest energy and enthusiasm, while muted or dark colors can indicate sadness or mystery. When selecting a color palette for your puppet, think about the emotions you want to evoke in your audience. A character designed for a children's show might utilize a bright and cheerful color scheme, while a more serious character in a dramatic performance might employ darker, more subdued tones. Texture also plays a significant role in character design. The materials used to create a puppet can influence how the audience perceives the character. A puppet made from soft, plush materials may appear warm and inviting, while one constructed from hard, metallic elements could seem cold and unapproachable. Consider how the texture of your puppet can enhance its personality and the story it tells. Proportions are essential in character design as well. Exaggerated features can create a sense of humor or whimsy, while realistic proportions may lend credibility to a character's role in a more serious narrative. Think about how the proportions of your puppet can reflect its personality. A character with oversized hands might suggest clumsiness or playfulness, while a character with elongated limbs could convey elegance or grace. Finally, the character's silhouette is crucial in making it recognizable and memorable. A strong silhouette can communicate a character's essence even from a distance. When designing your puppet, consider how its outline can convey its personality and role in the story. A distinctive silhouette can make your character stand out and be easily identifiable to the audience.

Visual Appeal

Visual appeal is a critical aspect of character design that can significantly impact how an audience engages with a puppet. A visually appealing character can draw the audience in, creating an immediate connection that enhances the overall experience of the performance. One way to enhance visual appeal is through the use of contrast. Contrast can be achieved through color, shape, and texture. For example, pairing a brightly colored puppet with a darker background can make the character pop, drawing the audience's attention. Similarly, contrasting textures—such as a smooth puppet against a rough backdrop—can create visual interest and depth. Another technique to enhance visual appeal is through the use of patterns. Patterns can add complexity and richness to a character's design, making it more engaging for the audience. Consider incorporating patterns into your puppet's costume or features, such as stripes, polka dots, or floral designs. These patterns can reflect the character's personality and add an extra layer of visual intrigue. Facial features are also vital in creating visual appeal. The eyes, mouth, and other facial elements are often the most expressive parts of a puppet. Designing expressive eyes can significantly enhance a character's visual appeal, as they can convey a wide range of emotions. Consider how the shape, size, and color of the eyes can reflect the character's personality. A character with large, round eyes may appear innocent and curious, while a character with narrow, slanted eyes might seem cunning or mischievous. The use of accessories can further enhance a puppet's visual appeal. Accessories such as hats, glasses, or jewelry can add personality and flair to a character's design. These elements can also serve to reinforce the character's backstory or role in the narrative. For instance, a character who is a wise old sage might wear glasses and carry a staff, while a playful child character might sport a colorful cap and oversized shoes. Finally, consider the overall composition of your puppet's design. The arrangement of colors, shapes, and features should create a harmonious and balanced look. A well-composed character design can be visually striking and memorable, leaving a lasting impression on the audience.

Emotional Connection

Creating an emotional connection between the audience and a puppet character is one of the most rewarding aspects of puppetry. When an audience feels a connection to a character, they become more invested in the story and the performance. This emotional bond can be cultivated through various design elements and performance techniques. One of the most effective ways to foster an emotional connection is through relatability. A character that embodies traits or experiences familiar to the audience can create a sense of empathy and understanding. When designing your puppet, consider how its personality and backstory can resonate with the audience. A character who faces challenges similar to those of the audience can evoke feelings of compassion and support. Facial expressions are crucial in establishing an emotional connection. The ability to convey a range of emotions through the puppet's face can significantly impact how the audience perceives the character. Consider how the design of the puppet's face can facilitate expressive movements. A puppet with articulated features can display a wide array of emotions, from joy to sorrow, allowing the audience to connect with the character on a deeper level. Movement is another essential aspect of creating an emotional connection. The way a puppet moves can convey its personality and emotional state. A character that moves with grace and fluidity may evoke feelings of elegance and poise, while a character that moves in a jerky or awkward manner might elicit laughter or sympathy. When designing your puppet, think about how its physicality can enhance its emotional expression. Storytelling is at the heart of puppetry, and the narrative can significantly influence the emotional connection between the audience and the character. A well-crafted story that highlights the character's struggles, triumphs, and growth can create a powerful bond with the audience. Consider how the character's journey can resonate with universal themes, such as love, friendship, or perseverance, to deepen the emotional impact of the performance. Finally, the use of music and sound can enhance the emotional connection between the audience and the puppet character. A carefully chosen musical score or sound effects can evoke specific feelings and set the tone for the performance. Consider how the auditory elements can complement the visual aspects of your puppet, creating a cohesive and immersive experience for the audience. In summary, the art of character design in puppetry is a rich and intricate process that involves a careful balance of various elements. By thoughtfully considering shape, color, texture, proportions, and silhouette, you can create a character that is not only visually appealing but also emotionally resonant. The journey of character creation is a delightful exploration of creativity and expression, inviting both the artist and the audience to engage in a shared experience that transcends the boundaries of the stage.

Chapter 4: Types of Puppets

Puppetry is a vibrant and multifaceted art form that encompasses a wide array of puppet types, each with its own unique characteristics, techniques, and expressive possibilities. Understanding the different types of puppets is essential for any puppeteer or aspiring artist, as it allows for a deeper appreciation of the craft and opens up a world of creative potential. In this chapter, we will explore three primary types of puppets: hand puppets, marionettes, and shadow puppets. Each section will delve into their distinct features, historical significance, and the artistry involved in their manipulation.

Hand Puppets

Hand puppets, often referred to as glove puppets, are perhaps the most accessible and widely recognized form of puppetry. These delightful creations are designed to be worn on the hand, allowing the puppeteer to control the puppet's movements and expressions with their fingers. The simplicity of hand puppets belies the depth of creativity they can inspire.

History and Evolution

The origins of hand puppetry can be traced back to ancient civilizations, where they served as both entertainment and storytelling devices. In cultures around the world, hand puppets have been used to convey moral lessons, entertain children, and even satirize political figures. From the traditional Italian "puppet shows" to the vibrant "bunraku" of Japan, hand puppets have evolved through the ages, adapting to the cultural contexts in which they are created.

Design and Construction

Creating a hand puppet involves a blend of artistry and craftsmanship. The design process begins with conceptualizing the character, considering its personality, backstory, and physical attributes. The materials used can vary widely, from fabric and felt to more unconventional materials like recycled plastics or paper mache.

Material	Characteristics	Common Uses
Fabric	Soft, flexible, and easy to manipulate	Children's puppets, educational puppetry
Felt	Durable, colorful, and lightweight	Storytelling puppets, craft projects
Paper Mache	Sturdy and can be molded into various shapes	Artistic puppets, larger installations
Recycled Materials	Eco-friendly and encourages creativity	Community projects, workshops

The construction process typically involves sewing or gluing the materials together to form the puppet's body, head, and limbs. The puppeteer's hand enters through the bottom of the puppet, allowing for a range of movements, from simple gestures to complex expressions.

Performance Techniques

The art of manipulating hand puppets requires practice and skill. A puppeteer must master the subtleties of movement, using their fingers to create lifelike gestures and expressions. Voice modulation is equally important, as the puppeteer must bring the character to life through speech. Engaging an audience with a hand puppet often involves a playful interplay of dialogue, humor, and emotion. The intimacy of hand puppetry allows for a direct connection with the audience, making it an ideal choice for storytelling, educational performances, and interactive theater.

Marionettes

Marionettes, often referred to as string puppets, are a captivating form of puppetry that employs a system of strings or wires to control the puppet's movements. This intricate method of manipulation allows for a high degree of precision and fluidity, enabling marionettes to perform complex actions and convey a wide range of emotions.

Historical Context

The history of marionettes is rich and varied, with roots in ancient cultures across Europe, Asia, and beyond. They have been used in theatrical performances, religious ceremonies, and folk traditions. The art of marionette manipulation reached its zenith during the Renaissance, when skilled puppeteers showcased their talents in grand theaters, captivating audiences with elaborate performances.

Construction and Design

Creating a marionette is a meticulous process that requires both artistic vision and technical skill. The design phase involves sketching the character and determining its size, proportions, and features.

Component	Function	Materials
Head	Facial expressions and character identity	Wood, plastic, clay
Body	Structure and movement	Wood, fabric, foam
Strings	Control and manipulation	Nylon, cotton, fishing line
Control Bar	Allows puppeteer to manipulate strings	Wood, metal

The head is often crafted with great attention to detail, as it serves as the focal point of the character. The body is constructed to allow for a range of movements, with joints that enable the marionette to bend and pose. The strings are carefully attached to various points on the puppet, allowing the puppeteer to create lifelike movements by pulling and releasing the strings.

Manipulation Techniques

Manipulating a marionette requires a unique set of skills, as the puppeteer must coordinate their movements with the strings to create fluid and natural actions. This often involves a delicate balance of tension and release, as the puppeteer guides the puppet through its performance. The use of space and stagecraft is crucial in marionette performances. The puppeteer must be aware of the puppet's positioning, ensuring that it interacts effectively with the environment and other characters. This form of puppetry often lends itself to more dramatic storytelling, with the potential for intricate choreography and elaborate scenes.

Shadow Puppets

Shadow puppetry is a mesmerizing form of puppetry that relies on the interplay of light and shadow to create captivating visual narratives. This ancient art form has been practiced in various cultures around the world, enchanting audiences with its ethereal beauty and storytelling potential.

Origins and Cultural Significance

Shadow puppetry has a rich history, with origins dating back to ancient China, India, and Indonesia. In these cultures, shadow puppets were used to convey moral lessons, entertain audiences, and celebrate cultural traditions. The art form has evolved over centuries, adapting to the cultural contexts in which it is practiced.

Design and Creation

Creating shadow puppets involves a unique blend of artistry and craftsmanship. The design process begins with conceptualizing the characters and their roles in the story.

Material	Characteristics	Common Uses
Leather	Durable and allows for intricate detailing	Traditional shadow puppetry
Cardboard	Lightweight and easy to cut	Educational projects,

Material	Characteristics	Common Uses
		workshops
Plastic	Flexible and can be molded into various shapes	Modern adaptations, performances

The puppets are typically crafted from materials that allow light to pass through, creating striking silhouettes against a light source. The puppeteer manipulates the puppets behind a screen, using their hands or rods to create movement and expression.

Performance Techniques

Shadow puppetry relies heavily on the manipulation of light and shadow to convey emotion and narrative. The puppeteer must be skilled in controlling the light source, the distance between the puppet and the screen, and the timing of movements to create a captivating performance. The storytelling aspect of shadow puppetry is often enhanced by the use of music and narration, creating an immersive experience for the audience. The combination of visual artistry and auditory elements allows for a rich tapestry of storytelling that transcends cultural boundaries.

Chapter 5: Developing a Character Concept

Brainstorming Ideas

In the enchanting realm of puppetry, the genesis of a character often begins with a spark of inspiration, a fleeting thought that dances in the mind like a marionette on strings. The process of brainstorming is an exhilarating journey, one that invites the puppeteer to explore the vast landscapes of imagination. It is here, in this fertile ground of creativity, that characters are born, each with their own unique essence and story to tell. To embark on this journey, one might start by reflecting on personal experiences, memories, or even dreams. What moments have shaped your understanding of the world? What emotions linger in your heart? These reflections can serve as a wellspring of ideas, providing a rich tapestry from which to draw. Consider jotting down words or phrases that resonate with you, allowing them to swirl and intermingle until a character begins to emerge. Another fruitful avenue for brainstorming is to observe the world around you. People-watching in a bustling café or strolling through a vibrant market can unveil a myriad of character possibilities. Notice the quirks, the mannerisms, the stories etched on the faces of those you encounter. Each individual is a universe unto themselves, and within their lives lie countless narratives waiting to be explored. Engaging in collaborative brainstorming sessions with fellow artists can also ignite the creative flame. Sharing ideas in a supportive environment fosters a sense of community and can lead to unexpected breakthroughs. Encourage each participant to contribute their unique perspectives, allowing the collective energy to shape and refine character concepts. As you delve deeper into the brainstorming process, consider utilizing visual aids. Mood boards, sketches, and collages can help crystallize your ideas, providing a tangible representation of your character's essence. These visual elements can serve as a source of inspiration, guiding your creative choices as you move forward in the character development process. Ultimately, the key to successful brainstorming lies in embracing the fluidity of creativity. Allow yourself to explore without judgment, to play with ideas and let them evolve organically. Remember that every character, no matter how whimsical or profound, begins as a mere thought—a flicker of imagination waiting to be brought to life.

Character Backstory

Once the initial ideas have taken shape, the next step in developing a character concept is to delve into the intricate tapestry of their backstory. A character's history is the foundation upon which their personality, motivations, and relationships are built. It is through their past experiences that they come to life, gaining depth and authenticity. Begin by asking yourself fundamental questions about your character's origins. Where were they born? What kind of environment did they grow up in? The answers to these questions can provide insight into their worldview and the values they hold dear. For instance, a character raised in a bustling city may possess a different outlook on life than one who grew up in a serene countryside setting. Consider the pivotal moments that have shaped your character's journey. These could be triumphs, tragedies, or transformative experiences that have left an indelible mark on their psyche. Perhaps they faced a significant loss that instilled in them a sense of resilience, or maybe they achieved a long-held dream that fueled their ambition. Each of these moments adds layers to their personality, creating a rich narrative that informs their actions and decisions. Relationships play a crucial role in character backstory as well. Who are the key figures in your character's life? Family members, friends, mentors, or even adversaries can all influence their development. Explore the dynamics of these relationships—are they supportive or strained? Do they inspire growth or foster conflict? Understanding these connections will help you craft a more nuanced character who resonates with audiences. As you weave together the threads of your character's backstory, consider how their past informs their present. What unresolved issues linger from their history? How do their experiences shape their goals and desires? A well-developed backstory not only enriches your character but also provides a framework for their actions and choices throughout your puppet performance. In the world of puppetry, where characters often embody exaggerated traits and emotions, the backstory serves as a grounding force. It allows audiences to connect with the character on a deeper level, fostering empathy and understanding. When a character's motivations are rooted in a compelling backstory, their journey becomes all the more engaging and relatable.

Defining Character Goals

With a solid understanding of your character's backstory, the next step is to define their goals. Goals are the driving force behind a character's actions, propelling them forward on their journey. Whether they are seeking love, revenge, knowledge, or redemption, these aspirations shape the narrative and provide a sense of direction. Begin by identifying your character's primary goal. What is it that they desire most? This goal should be clear and compelling, serving as the anchor for their journey. For example, a character who longs to reunite with a lost loved one may be driven by a deep sense of longing and nostalgia, while another character seeking to prove their worth may be fueled by ambition and determination. Once the primary goal is established, consider the secondary goals that may arise along the way. These can add complexity to your character's journey, creating opportunities for growth and transformation. Perhaps your character's quest for love leads them to discover their own self-worth, or their pursuit of knowledge unveils hidden truths about their past. These secondary goals can serve as stepping stones, enriching the narrative and allowing for character development. It is also essential to explore the obstacles that stand in the way of your character's goals. What challenges must they overcome? These obstacles can take many forms—internal conflicts, external adversaries, or societal constraints. By introducing hurdles, you create tension and drama, keeping audiences engaged as they root for your character's success. As your character navigates their journey, consider how their goals may evolve. Characters are not static; they grow and change in response to their experiences. A character who begins with a singular focus may find their priorities shifting as they encounter new challenges and relationships. This evolution adds depth to their arc, making their journey all the more compelling. In the realm of puppetry, where emotions are often amplified, the clarity of a character's goals can resonate powerfully with audiences. When viewers understand what a character is striving for, they become invested in their journey, cheering for their triumphs and empathizing with their struggles.

Chapter 6: Personality Traits and Archetypes

The world of puppetry is a vibrant tapestry woven from the threads of imagination, creativity, and the rich spectrum of human emotion. At the heart of this art form lies the characters we create, each one a unique embodiment of personality traits and archetypes. Understanding these elements is essential for any puppeteer seeking to breathe life into their creations. This chapter delves into the intricacies of personality traits, the significance of archetypes, and the delicate balance required to craft compelling puppet characters that resonate with audiences.

Common Archetypes

Archetypes serve as foundational blueprints for character creation, providing a framework that resonates universally across cultures and narratives. These archetypes are not merely stereotypes; they are deeply rooted in the collective consciousness, allowing audiences to connect with characters on a profound level. One of the most recognizable archetypes is the Hero, often characterized by bravery, determination, and a quest for justice. This character embarks on a journey, facing challenges that test their resolve and ultimately lead to personal growth. In puppetry, the Hero can take many forms, from a valiant knight to a humble farmer, each with their own unique story and struggles. In contrast, the Villain archetype embodies traits such as cunning, ambition, and a desire for power. Villains are essential to storytelling, providing conflict and tension that propel the narrative forward. A puppet villain can be both fearsome and comical, allowing for a range of interpretations that keep audiences engaged. The Mentor archetype plays a crucial role in guiding the Hero, often imparting wisdom and knowledge. This character is typically wise, experienced, and nurturing, serving as a beacon of hope and guidance. In puppetry, the Mentor can be portrayed as a wise old sage or a quirky, eccentric figure, each bringing their own flavor to the character. Another common archetype is the Trickster, known for their playful and mischievous nature. Tricksters challenge the status quo, often using humor and wit to navigate complex situations. In puppetry, this archetype can be particularly engaging, as the Trickster's antics can elicit laughter while also delivering deeper messages about life and society. The Innocent archetype represents purity, optimism, and a desire for happiness. This character often serves as a foil to darker elements in the story, reminding audiences of the beauty and simplicity of life. In puppetry, the Innocent can be depicted as a childlike figure, embodying wonder and curiosity. Lastly, the Shadow archetype represents the darker aspects of the human psyche, often manifesting as fear, jealousy, or unresolved conflict. This character can serve as a powerful catalyst for growth and transformation, challenging the Hero to confront their inner demons. In puppetry, the Shadow can be represented through dark, foreboding designs and movements that evoke a sense of unease. These archetypes are not rigid categories but rather fluid concepts that can be blended and reinterpreted. Puppeteers have the creative freedom to mix traits from different archetypes, creating characters that are multifaceted and relatable. By understanding these common archetypes, puppeteers can craft characters that resonate with audiences, drawing them into the narrative and evoking a range of emotions.

Creating Unique Personalities

While archetypes provide a solid foundation, the true magic of puppetry lies in the creation of unique personalities that breathe life into these archetypal frameworks. To develop a distinctive character, puppeteers must delve into the nuances of personality traits, motivations, and experiences that shape their puppets. One effective approach to creating unique personalities is to consider the Five Factor Model of personality, which encompasses openness, conscientiousness, extraversion, agreeableness, and neuroticism. Each of these traits can be manipulated to create a rich tapestry of character depth. For example, a puppet that scores high on openness may be adventurous and curious, eager to explore new ideas and experiences. In contrast, a character low in openness may be more traditional and resistant to change, providing a compelling dynamic within the story. Another essential aspect of personality development is understanding a character's motivations. What drives your puppet? Is it a desire for acceptance, a quest for knowledge, or perhaps a longing for revenge? By identifying a character's core motivations, puppeteers can create a more authentic and relatable persona. This depth of character allows audiences to connect emotionally, fostering empathy and investment in the puppet's journey. Backstory is another critical element in crafting unique personalities. Every character has a history that shapes who they are in the present. By developing a rich backstory, puppeteers can inform their character's decisions, fears, and desires. For instance, a puppet who grew up in a nurturing environment may exhibit traits of kindness and generosity, while one who faced adversity may display resilience and a hardened exterior. Additionally, consider the quirks and idiosyncrasies that make a character memorable. These can range from a unique way of speaking to peculiar habits or mannerisms. A puppet that twirls its hair when nervous or speaks in rhymes can stand out in the minds of the audience, adding layers of charm and relatability. Furthermore, the interplay of relationships can significantly influence a character's personality. How does your puppet interact with others? Are they a natural leader, a loyal friend, or a solitary figure? The dynamics between characters can reveal much about their personalities and create opportunities for growth and conflict. In puppetry, the visual representation of a character also plays a vital role in conveying personality. The design, colors, and materials used in a puppet can reflect its traits and emotions. A bright, colorful puppet may exude joy and energy, while a darker, more muted design may suggest mystery or sadness. Puppeteers should consider how these visual elements align with the character's personality, creating a cohesive and engaging representation. Ultimately, the goal of creating unique personalities is to craft characters that feel real and relatable, allowing audiences to see themselves in the puppets' journeys. By blending archetypes with individual traits, motivations, and backstories, puppeteers can create a diverse cast of characters that resonate on multiple levels.

Balancing Traits

Creating compelling puppet characters involves not only the selection of traits but also the delicate balance between them. A well-rounded character should embody a mix of strengths and weaknesses, allowing for growth and development throughout the narrative. One approach to achieving balance is to consider the dualities present within a character. For instance, a puppet may be both brave and fearful, showcasing the internal struggle between courage and vulnerability. This complexity adds depth to the character, making them more relatable and human. Audiences often connect with characters who grapple with their flaws, as it mirrors the challenges faced in real life. Another essential aspect of balancing traits is the concept of conflict. Characters should face internal and external conflicts that challenge their beliefs and push them to evolve. A puppet that is overly confident may encounter situations that test their abilities, forcing them to confront their limitations. Conversely, a character with low self-esteem may be presented with opportunities that challenge them to step outside their comfort zone. This interplay of strengths and weaknesses creates a dynamic narrative arc that keeps audiences engaged. Additionally, consider the relationships between characters when balancing traits. A puppet's personality can be amplified or softened in response to others. For example, a character who is typically shy may find their voice when paired with a more extroverted puppet, creating a harmonious balance that enhances both personalities. This dynamic can lead to moments of humor, tension, and growth, enriching the overall narrative. It is also crucial to recognize the context in which a character operates. The environment and circumstances surrounding a puppet can influence their behavior and traits. A character may exhibit bravery in a familiar setting but falter in an unfamiliar one. By considering the context, puppeteers can create characters that feel authentic and responsive to their surroundings. Moreover, the evolution of traits throughout the story is vital for character development. Characters should not remain static; they must grow and change in response to their experiences. A puppet that begins as timid may gradually gain confidence through challenges, while a once arrogant character may learn humility through failure. This journey of transformation adds richness to the narrative and allows audiences to witness the characters' growth. Finally, it is essential to ensure that the balance of traits aligns with the overall theme of the puppet show. Each character should contribute to the central message, whether it be about friendship, courage, or the importance of embracing one's true self. By maintaining this thematic coherence, puppeteers can create a harmonious ensemble of characters that resonate with audiences on a deeper level.

Chapter 7: Physical Attributes of Puppets

The physical attributes of puppets serve as the foundation upon which character and narrative are built. These attributes are not merely aesthetic; they are essential in conveying personality, emotion, and intention. In this chapter, we will explore the intricacies of size and shape, color schemes, and material choices that contribute to the overall character design of puppets.

Size and Shape

The size and shape of a puppet play a crucial role in how it is perceived by the audience. A puppet's dimensions can evoke specific feelings and associations, influencing the audience's emotional response. For instance, larger puppets often command attention and can symbolize authority or power, while smaller puppets may evoke intimacy or vulnerability. When considering size, it is essential to think about the context in which the puppet will be used. A puppet designed for a stage performance may differ significantly in size from one intended for close-up interactions in a workshop setting. The scale must be appropriate for the intended audience and the environment. Shape is equally significant. The contours and forms of a puppet can suggest various traits. A puppet with rounded shapes may appear friendly and approachable, while angular shapes might convey sharpness or aggression. The silhouette of a puppet can also communicate its role in the story. For example, a whimsical character might have exaggerated features, such as oversized heads or elongated limbs, to enhance its playful nature. In the realm of puppetry, the interplay between size and shape can create a dynamic visual language. A puppet with a large head and small body may suggest a childlike innocence, while a tall, slender puppet could represent elegance or aloofness. Consider the classic character of Big Bird from "Sesame Street." His towering height and round, soft shape create an image of warmth and friendliness, making him an ideal character for engaging with children. In contrast, the sharp angles and smaller stature of a character like Elmo convey a different kind of energy—one that is playful yet slightly mischievous. The choice of size and shape should also reflect the character's personality and role within the narrative. A villainous character might be designed with a more imposing size and jagged shapes to instill fear, while a hero may have a balanced and proportionate form that embodies strength and reliability.

Color Schemes

Color is a powerful tool in character design, capable of evoking emotions and setting the tone for a puppet's personality. The choice of colors can significantly influence how an audience perceives a character, making it essential to consider color schemes carefully. Colors can be categorized into warm and cool tones, each carrying its own emotional weight. Warm colors, such as reds, oranges, and yellows, often evoke feelings of excitement, energy, and warmth. These colors can be particularly effective for characters that are lively, enthusiastic, or passionate. For instance, a puppet designed to be a cheerful and optimistic character might feature bright yellows and oranges, instantly drawing the audience's attention and creating a sense of joy. On the other hand, cool colors like blues, greens, and purples tend to convey calmness, serenity, and introspection. These colors can be used to create characters that are thoughtful, wise, or even melancholic. A puppet representing a wise old sage might be adorned in deep blues and purples, suggesting depth and contemplation. The combination of colors can also create striking contrasts that enhance a puppet's visual appeal. A character with a predominantly dark color palette can be accentuated with bright, contrasting colors to draw attention to specific features or expressions. For example, a puppet with a dark cloak might have a vibrant red scarf, symbolizing passion or danger. Moreover, cultural associations with colors should not be overlooked. Different cultures may attribute various meanings to specific colors, which can influence how a puppet is perceived. For instance, while white is often associated with purity in Western cultures, it may symbolize mourning in some Eastern cultures. Understanding these nuances can enrich the character's design and deepen its connection with the audience. In addition to the emotional impact of colors, the use of patterns can add complexity to a puppet's design. Stripes, polka dots, or floral patterns can suggest playfulness or whimsy, while more subdued patterns may convey sophistication or elegance. Consider the character of Kermit the Frog. His vibrant green color not only makes him instantly recognizable but also embodies a sense of freshness and vitality. The simplicity of his design, combined with the bright color, allows him to connect with audiences of all ages, making him a beloved figure in the world of puppetry.

Material Choices

The materials used in puppet construction are vital in shaping both the puppet's physical attributes and its overall character. The choice of materials can affect the puppet's weight, texture, and durability, all of which contribute to its performance capabilities and visual appeal. Traditional puppetry often employs materials such as wood, cloth, and foam. Each material brings its own unique qualities to the puppet. For instance, wooden puppets can have a sturdy and classic feel, often associated with marionettes. The natural grain of the wood can add character and warmth, while the weight allows for precise control during performances. Cloth puppets, on the other hand, offer a softer, more approachable aesthetic. They can be easily manipulated and are often used in children's puppetry due to their friendly appearance. The texture of the fabric can also enhance the character's personality; for example, a puppet made from fuzzy fabric may appear cuddly and inviting, while a puppet made from shiny satin could suggest elegance or flamboyance. Foam is another popular material in puppet construction, especially for characters requiring exaggerated features or lightweight designs. Foam puppets can be easily shaped and painted, allowing for creative freedom in character design. The lightweight nature of foam also enables performers to manipulate the puppets with ease, enhancing the overall performance experience. In recent years, advancements in technology have introduced new materials such as silicone and 3D-printed components into the world of puppetry. These materials offer unique possibilities for character design, allowing for intricate details and lifelike movements. Silicone puppets, for instance, can mimic human skin, providing a realistic appearance that can enhance emotional expression. The choice of materials should also consider the puppet's intended use. A puppet designed for outdoor performances may require more durable materials to withstand the elements, while a puppet for indoor use might prioritize aesthetics over durability. Additionally, the environmental impact of material choices is becoming increasingly important in contemporary puppetry. Many artists are exploring sustainable materials and practices, creating puppets that not only tell stories but also reflect a commitment to environmental stewardship.

Chapter 8: Voice and Speech Patterns

The art of puppetry transcends mere visual representation; it is a symphony of sound and movement that breathes life into inanimate objects. The voice of a puppet is not just an accessory; it is the very essence of its character. The way a puppet speaks can evoke laughter, empathy, or even fear. In this chapter, we will explore the intricacies of creating distinct voices, employing various speech techniques, and utilizing accents to enhance the depth and authenticity of your puppet characters.

Creating Distinct Voices

The first step in crafting a puppet's voice is to understand the character's personality and background. A voice should reflect the essence of the character, capturing their unique traits and quirks. Here are some key considerations when developing a distinct voice for your puppet:

1. Character Background

The history and background of your puppet will significantly influence its voice. Consider the following questions:

- What is the puppet's age?

- Where does it come from?

- What experiences have shaped its personality?

For instance, a wise old sage might have a slow, deliberate voice, filled with gravitas, while a mischievous child character could have a high-pitched, rapid-fire delivery.

2. Emotional Range

A puppet's voice should be versatile enough to convey a range of emotions. Think about how your character would express joy, sadness, anger, or surprise. Experiment with pitch, volume, and pacing to find the right vocal quality that aligns with the emotional state of your puppet.

3. Vocal Techniques

Utilizing various vocal techniques can help differentiate your puppet's voice. Here are some techniques to consider:

- Vocal Modulation: Change the pitch and tone of your voice to create different characters. A deep, resonant voice can convey authority, while a squeaky, high-pitched voice can suggest innocence or playfulness.

- Vocal Effects: Incorporate effects such as whispers, growls, or even exaggerated accents to add depth to your puppet's voice.

- Character-Specific Sounds: Some characters may have unique sounds or catch phrases that become their signature. Think of how Kermit the Frog has his distinctive "Hi-ho!"

Speech Techniques

Once you have established a distinct voice for your puppet, the next step is to refine the speech techniques that will bring that voice to life. The way a puppet articulates words can enhance its personality and make it more relatable to the audience.

1. Pacing and Rhythm

The pacing of speech is crucial in puppetry. A character that speaks quickly may come across as anxious or excited, while a slower pace can suggest thoughtfulness or seriousness. Consider the following aspects:

- Pauses: Strategic pauses can add dramatic effect or emphasize a point. A well-timed pause can create anticipation or allow the audience to absorb a punchline.

- Rhythm: The rhythm of speech can be influenced by the character's background. For example, a character from a musical background may have a lyrical quality to their speech, while a more straightforward character may have a staccato rhythm.

2. Articulation and Clarity

Clear articulation is essential for effective communication. Puppets should be able to pronounce words distinctly, ensuring that the audience can understand them. Here are some tips for improving articulation:

- Practice Tongue Twisters: Engaging in tongue twisters can help improve clarity and precision in speech.

- Vocal Warm-Ups: Just like actors, puppeteers should warm up their voices before performances. This can include humming, lip trills, and vocal exercises to enhance flexibility.

3. Emotional Inflection

Infusing emotion into speech is vital for connecting with the audience. A puppet's voice should reflect its feelings and intentions. Consider the following techniques:

- Vocal Dynamics: Varying the volume and intensity of speech can convey different emotions. A soft, gentle tone may express tenderness, while a loud, booming voice can indicate anger or excitement.

- Emphasis: Placing emphasis on certain words can change the meaning of a sentence. Experiment with which words to stress to convey the intended emotion effectively.

Using Accents

Accents can add an additional layer of depth to your puppet characters, making them more relatable and engaging. However, it is essential to approach the use of accents with sensitivity and respect.

1. Research and Authenticity

When incorporating an accent, thorough research is crucial. Understanding the nuances of an accent can help you portray it authentically. Consider the following:

- Listen and Imitate: Spend time listening to native speakers of the accent you wish to portray. Pay attention to the rhythm, intonation, and specific sounds that characterize the accent.

- Cultural Context: Be aware of the cultural context surrounding the accent. Ensure that your portrayal is respectful and does not perpetuate stereotypes.

2. Practice and Refinement

Accents require practice to master. Here are some strategies to refine your accent skills:

- Record and Playback: Record yourself speaking in the accent and listen to the playback. This can help you identify areas for improvement.

- Accent Coaches: Consider working with an accent coach or taking classes to enhance your skills. Professional guidance can provide valuable insights and techniques.

3. Integrating Accents into Character Development

When using accents, it is essential to integrate them into the character's overall development. An accent should feel like a natural extension of the character's identity. Consider the following:

- Character Consistency: Ensure that the accent aligns with the character's background and personality. A sophisticated character may have a refined accent, while a street-smart character may have a more casual tone.

- Audience Connection: Accents can help establish a connection with the audience. A relatable accent can make a character feel more approachable and engaging.

Table of Vocal Techniques

Technique	Description	Example
Vocal Modulation	Changing pitch and tone to create different characters.	A deep voice for a villain, a high-pitched voice for a child.
Vocal Effects	Incorporating unique sounds or catchphrases.	Using a growl for a monster character.
Pacing and Rhythm	Adjusting speed and flow of speech.	Quick speech for excitement, slow for seriousness.
Emotional Inflection	Varying volume and emphasis to convey emotions.	Soft tone for tenderness, loud for anger.
Accents	Using regional or cultural accents to enhance character.	A British accent for a sophisticated character.

Chapter 9: Movement and Expression

The art of puppetry transcends mere manipulation of inanimate objects; it is a dance of spirit and form, a celebration of life through the medium of crafted characters. In this chapter, we delve into the intricate relationship between movement and expression, exploring how these elements breathe life into puppets, allowing them to resonate with audiences on a profound level.

Body Language

Body language is the silent language of the puppet, conveying emotions and intentions without uttering a single word. Just as in human communication, the subtleties of posture, gesture, and spatial awareness play a pivotal role in how a character is perceived. A puppet's body language can express a wide array of feelings, from joy and excitement to sadness and despair. To master body language in puppetry, one must first understand the anatomy of the puppet itself. Each type of puppet—be it a marionette, hand puppet, or shadow puppet—has its own unique capabilities and limitations. For instance, a marionette, with its strings and joints, can achieve a fluidity of movement that allows for graceful gestures, while a hand puppet may rely more heavily on the puppeteer's dexterity and creativity to convey emotion. Consider the way a puppet stands. A character that is confident may have a straight posture, with shoulders back and head held high, while a timid character might hunch over, avoiding eye contact. The positioning of limbs can also communicate a wealth of information. Outstretched arms can signify openness or excitement, while crossed arms may suggest defensiveness or reluctance. Moreover, the concept of personal space is crucial in puppetry. Just as humans have varying comfort levels with proximity, so too do puppets. A puppet that invades another character's personal space may be perceived as aggressive or overly familiar, while one that maintains a respectful distance may come across as polite or reserved. Incorporating these nuances into your puppet's body language requires keen observation of human interactions. Spend time watching people in various settings—how they stand, how they gesture, and how they react to one another. This practice will enrich your understanding of non-verbal communication, allowing you to translate those observations into your puppetry.

Gesture and Movement

The gestures of a puppet can be both exaggerated and subtle, depending on the character's personality and the context of the performance. Exaggerated movements can heighten comedic moments or emphasize dramatic tension, while subtle gestures can create intimacy and connection with the audience. For instance, a puppet that is excited might bounce on its feet, flail its arms, and exhibit rapid head movements, while a puppet that is contemplative may move slowly, with deliberate hand gestures that reflect its inner thoughts. The rhythm of movement is equally important; a fast-paced character may dart around the stage, while a more languid character may take its time, savoring each step. In addition to the physicality of gestures, the intention behind them is paramount. A wave can signify a greeting, farewell, or even a dismissive gesture, depending on the accompanying facial expression and context. Understanding the emotional weight of gestures allows puppeteers to create multi-dimensional characters that resonate with audiences.

Spatial Awareness

Spatial awareness is another critical aspect of body language in puppetry. Puppets must navigate their environment with a sense of purpose and intention. This involves not only the physical space they occupy but also their relationship to other characters and objects on stage. A puppet that moves purposefully through space conveys confidence and agency, while one that hesitates or stumbles may evoke sympathy or uncertainty. The use of levels—such as having a puppet climb, jump, or crouch—can also add depth to the performance, creating visual interest and enhancing the narrative. Furthermore, the interaction between puppets can be a powerful tool for storytelling. The way one puppet reacts to another's movements can reveal their relationship dynamics. For example, a puppet that steps back in response to another's advance may indicate fear or submission, while one that leans in may express curiosity or affection.

Facial Expressions

Facial expressions are the windows to a puppet's soul, allowing audiences to connect with characters on an emotional level. While puppets may lack the intricate musculature of human faces, skilled puppeteers can create a wide range of expressions through careful manipulation of the puppet's features. The eyes, in particular, are crucial in conveying emotion. A puppet with wide-open eyes can express surprise or excitement, while narrowed eyes may suggest suspicion or anger. The direction in which a puppet's eyes gaze can also indicate focus or distraction, guiding the audience's attention to key moments in the performance. Mouth movements play an equally important role in expressing emotion. A puppet that smiles can radiate joy, while a frown can evoke sadness or frustration. The shape of the mouth can also convey nuances; a puppet with a slight smirk may suggest mischief or sarcasm, while a wide-open mouth can signify shock or awe. To enhance facial expressions, puppeteers can utilize various techniques, such as changing the angle of the puppet's head or adjusting the position of its features. For instance, tilting the head slightly can create a sense of curiosity or confusion, while a downward gaze may indicate shame or defeat.

Creating Emotional Resonance

To create emotional resonance through facial expressions, puppeteers must tap into their own emotional experiences. Reflecting on personal moments of joy, sorrow, or anger can inform the way a puppet expresses these feelings. This authenticity translates into a more relatable performance, allowing audiences to empathize with the character's journey. Additionally, the use of props and costumes can enhance facial expressions. A puppet adorned with vibrant colors and whimsical accessories may evoke a sense of playfulness, while one dressed in muted tones may convey seriousness or melancholy. The interplay between a puppet's appearance and its expressions creates a rich tapestry of storytelling possibilities.

Facial Manipulation Techniques

Various techniques can be employed to manipulate a puppet's facial features effectively. For instance, using a combination of levers and springs can allow for dynamic mouth movements, enabling the puppet to "speak" in sync with the puppeteer's voice. Similarly, employing mechanisms that allow for eye movement can create a more lifelike presence, as the puppet can "look" at other characters or objects on stage. Puppeteers can also experiment with different materials to create expressive faces. Soft fabrics may lend themselves to a more whimsical appearance, while rigid materials can convey a sense of seriousness or authority. The choice of materials can significantly impact how audiences perceive a character's emotions.

Movement Techniques

Movement techniques in puppetry are the lifeblood of a performance, infusing characters with vitality and dynamism. The way a puppet moves can define its personality, establish relationships, and drive the narrative forward. One fundamental movement technique is the concept of "weight." A puppet that embodies a heavy, lumbering presence may move slowly and deliberately, while a light, agile character may dart around with ease. Understanding the weight of a puppet allows the puppeteer to create movements that feel authentic and believable.

Timing and Rhythm

Timing and rhythm are essential components of movement in puppetry. The pacing of a puppet's actions can heighten comedic moments, build tension, or create a sense of anticipation. For instance, a well-timed pause before a punchline can amplify the humor, while a slow, deliberate movement can create suspense before a climactic moment. Incorporating rhythm into movement can also enhance the overall performance. A puppet that moves in sync with music or sound effects can create a harmonious experience for the audience, drawing them deeper into the narrative. The interplay between movement and sound can evoke a range of emotions, from joy to melancholy.

Choreography and Blocking

Choreography and blocking are vital aspects of puppetry that dictate how characters interact with one another and their environment. Thoughtful choreography ensures that movements are purposeful and contribute to the storytelling. This may involve planning specific gestures, entrances, and exits that align with the narrative arc. Blocking, or the positioning of puppets on stage, is equally important. A well-blocked scene allows for clear sightlines and ensures that the audience can fully engage with the performance. Consideration of spatial relationships between characters can enhance the emotional impact of their interactions, creating a more immersive experience.

Improvisation in Movement

Improvisation is a powerful tool in puppetry, allowing puppeteers to respond to the energy of the moment and adapt their movements accordingly. Embracing spontaneity can lead to unexpected and delightful moments that resonate with audiences. Puppeteers can practice improvisational techniques by engaging in exercises that encourage free movement and exploration. This may involve setting up scenarios and allowing the puppet to react organically, fostering a sense of playfulness and creativity. Incorporating improvisation into rehearsals can also strengthen the bond between the puppeteer and the puppet, as they learn to communicate and respond to one another in real-time. This synergy enhances the overall performance, creating a captivating experience for the audience. As we explore the intricate dance of movement and expression in puppetry, we uncover the profound impact these elements have on character creation. Through body language, facial expressions, and movement techniques, puppeteers can craft characters that resonate deeply with audiences, inviting them into a world of imagination and emotion. The journey of puppetry is one of discovery, where each movement and expression becomes a brushstroke on the canvas of storytelling, painting a vivid picture of life, laughter, and connection.

Chapter 10: Crafting a Puppet's Backstory

The world of puppetry is a vibrant tapestry woven from threads of creativity, emotion, and storytelling. At the heart of every puppet lies a character, and at the heart of every character lies a backstory. Crafting a puppet's backstory is not merely an exercise in imagination; it is an essential component that breathes life into the puppet, allowing it to resonate with audiences on a profound level.

Backstory serves as the foundation upon which a character is built, providing context for their actions, motivations, and relationships. It is the narrative that informs the puppet's personality, quirks, and emotional depth. In this chapter, we will explore the significance of backstory, how to integrate history into character creation, and the motivations and conflicts that shape a puppet's journey.

Importance of Backstory

Backstory is the hidden narrative that shapes a character's present. It encompasses the experiences, relationships, and events that have influenced the puppet's development. Just as a well-crafted novel or film relies on character backstories to engage the audience, puppetry thrives on the richness of its characters' histories.

A puppet without a backstory is akin to a blank canvas; it may be visually appealing, but it lacks the depth and intrigue that draws viewers in. By crafting a compelling backstory, puppeteers can create characters that evoke empathy, laughter, and reflection.

Consider the classic puppet archetypes: the wise old sage, the mischievous trickster, or the innocent child. Each of these characters carries a backstory that informs their behavior and interactions. The wise old sage may have endured a lifetime of trials, gaining wisdom through hardship. The trickster might have a history of clever escapades that shape their playful nature. The innocent child could be a reflection of lost innocence, yearning for connection in a chaotic world.

When developing a puppet's backstory, it is essential to consider the following elements:

1. Origins: Where did the character come from? What is their cultural background? Understanding the origins of a puppet can provide insight into their worldview and behavior.

2. Key Events: What significant events have shaped the character's life? These moments can serve as turning points that define the puppet's personality and choices.

3. Relationships: Who are the important figures in the puppet's life? Relationships with family, friends, and adversaries can add layers of complexity to the character.

4. Goals and Aspirations: What does the puppet desire? Understanding their goals can drive the narrative and create opportunities for conflict and growth.

By thoughtfully considering these elements, puppeteers can create rich, multi-dimensional characters that resonate with audiences, inviting them to invest emotionally in the puppet's journey.

Integrating History

History is a powerful tool in character creation, providing context and depth to a puppet's backstory. Integrating historical elements into a puppet's narrative can enhance its authenticity and relatability.

When crafting a puppet's history, consider the broader cultural and societal influences that may have shaped the character. For instance, a puppet representing a historical figure or cultural icon can draw from real events and experiences, grounding its narrative in reality. This approach not only enriches the character but also offers audiences a glimpse into the past, fostering a deeper connection to the puppet's story.

Moreover, integrating history can involve exploring the traditions and folklore of different cultures. Puppetry has a rich history across the globe, with each culture contributing unique styles, themes, and characters. By incorporating elements from various traditions, puppeteers can create characters that reflect a diverse range of experiences and perspectives.

For example, a puppet inspired by the folklore of a specific region might embody the values and beliefs of that culture. This character could navigate challenges that resonate with the audience, drawing parallels between the puppet's journey and their own experiences.

Additionally, historical events can serve as a backdrop for a puppet's story. A puppet created to represent a time of social change or upheaval can engage audiences in conversations about relevant issues, making the performance not only entertaining but also thought-provoking.

Incorporating history into a puppet's backstory requires careful research and consideration. Puppeteers should strive to portray historical elements accurately and respectfully, ensuring that the character's narrative honors the cultures and experiences it represents.

Motivations and Conflicts

At the core of every compelling story lies conflict, and the same holds true for puppetry. A puppet's motivations and conflicts drive the narrative, creating tension and engagement for the audience. Understanding what motivates a puppet and the challenges it faces is crucial for crafting a captivating backstory.

Motivations are the desires and goals that propel a character forward. They can range from simple wants, such as seeking friendship or adventure, to more complex aspirations, such as striving for justice or redemption. A puppet's motivations should be clear and relatable, allowing the audience to empathize with its journey.

For instance, a puppet that yearns for acceptance may face conflicts that challenge its self-worth. This struggle can resonate with audiences who have experienced similar feelings of isolation or rejection. By portraying these motivations authentically, puppeteers can create characters that evoke genuine emotional responses.

Conflicts, on the other hand, are the obstacles that stand in the way of a puppet's goals. These challenges can be external, such as a rival character or societal expectations, or internal, such as self-doubt or fear. The interplay between motivations and conflicts creates a dynamic narrative arc, allowing the puppet to grow and evolve throughout the story.

Consider a puppet character who dreams of becoming a great artist but grapples with self-doubt and criticism from others. This internal conflict can lead to moments of vulnerability and resilience, showcasing the character's journey toward self-acceptance and fulfillment.

In crafting a puppet's motivations and conflicts, puppeteers should aim for authenticity and relatability. Audiences are drawn to characters that reflect their own struggles and aspirations, making it essential to create a backstory that resonates on a personal level.

Ultimately, the backstory of a puppet is a tapestry of experiences, emotions, and aspirations. By weaving together the threads of history, motivations, and conflicts, puppeteers can create characters that are not only entertaining but also deeply meaningful. These characters invite audiences to embark on a journey of discovery, reflection, and connection, reminding us of the power of storytelling through the art of puppetry.

Chapter 11: The Role of Humor in Puppetry

Humor is a universal language that transcends barriers, and in the realm of puppetry, it serves as a powerful tool for connection and engagement. The art of puppetry, with its unique blend of visual storytelling and character interaction, provides a fertile ground for humor to flourish. This chapter delves into the various dimensions of humor in puppetry, exploring its types, the nuances of timing and delivery, and the intricacies of creating comedic characters.

Types of Humor

Humor can take many forms, each with its own charm and appeal. Understanding the different types of humor can help puppeteers craft performances that resonate with their audiences. Below are some of the most prevalent types of humor found in puppetry:

Type of Humor	Description	Examples in Puppetry
Slapstick	Physical comedy that involves exaggerated movements and situations.	Characters tripping, falling, or engaging in absurdly exaggerated fights.
Wordplay	Humor that relies on clever language, puns, and double meanings.	Characters engaging in witty banter or clever repartee.
Satire	Humor that critiques or mocks societal norms, politics, or cultural phenomena.	Puppets parodying politicians or social issues in a humorous light.
Character Humor	Humor derived from the quirks and idiosyncrasies of a character.	A puppet with a peculiar laugh or an exaggerated personality trait.
Situational Humor	Humor that arises from the context or situation in which characters find themselves.	Puppets caught in absurd or unexpected scenarios.

Type of Humor	Description	Examples in Puppetry
Dark Humor	Humor that finds comedy in serious or taboo subjects.	Puppets addressing heavy themes with a light-hearted twist.

Each type of humor can be employed strategically to enhance the narrative and engage the audience. For instance, slapstick humor often appeals to younger audiences, while satire may resonate more with adults. The key is to know your audience and tailor your comedic approach accordingly.

Timing and Delivery

In the world of comedy, timing is everything. The effectiveness of a joke or humorous moment often hinges on the precise moment it is delivered. In puppetry, this is particularly crucial, as the puppeteer must synchronize their movements, voice, and timing to create a seamless comedic experience. Here are some essential elements to consider regarding timing and delivery:

1. Pacing

The pace at which humor is delivered can significantly impact its effectiveness. A well-timed pause before a punchline can heighten anticipation and amplify laughter. Conversely, rushing through a joke can lead to missed opportunities for humor. Puppeteers should practice their timing, ensuring that each comedic moment is given the space it needs to breathe.

2. Physical Timing

In puppetry, physicality plays a vital role in humor. The timing of a puppet's movements, gestures, and expressions can enhance comedic moments. For example, a puppet that dramatically pauses before a silly action can create a humorous contrast that elicits laughter. Puppeteers should experiment with different physical timings to discover what works best for their characters.

3. Vocal Delivery

The voice of a puppet is a crucial component of its comedic identity. The tone, pitch, and rhythm of a puppet's speech can add layers of humor. A character with a high-pitched, squeaky voice may deliver absurd lines in a way that amplifies their comedic effect. Puppeteers should explore various vocal styles and techniques to find the perfect fit for their characters.

4. Audience Interaction

Engaging with the audience can create spontaneous comedic moments. Puppeteers can incorporate audience reactions into their performances, responding to laughter or gasps in real-time. This interaction not only enhances the humor but also fosters a sense of connection between the puppeteer, the puppets, and the audience.

Creating Comedic Characters

The foundation of humor in puppetry often lies in the characters themselves. Crafting comedic characters requires a thoughtful approach that considers their personality, quirks, and relationships with other characters. Here are some key elements to keep in mind when creating comedic characters:

1. Defining Character Traits

Every comedic character should have distinct traits that contribute to their humor. These traits can be exaggerated versions of real-life characteristics or entirely fantastical attributes. For example, a character who is overly optimistic in the face of absurdity can create humor through their unwavering positivity. Puppeteers should brainstorm and define their characters' traits to establish a solid comedic foundation.

2. Relationships and Dynamics

The interactions between characters can generate humor through conflict, misunderstandings, or camaraderie. A comedic duo, for instance, may consist of a straight man and a jokester, where the straight man's serious demeanor amplifies the humor of the jokester's antics. Puppeteers should explore the dynamics between their characters, considering how their relationships can enhance comedic moments.

3. Visual Design

The visual appearance of a puppet can contribute significantly to its comedic identity. Exaggerated features, vibrant colors, and whimsical designs can evoke laughter even before a word is spoken. A puppet with oversized glasses or an absurd hairstyle can immediately signal to the audience that humor is at play. Puppeteers should collaborate with designers to create visually striking and humorous characters.

4. Backstory and Motivation

A character's backstory can inform their comedic behavior. Understanding why a character behaves in a certain way can add depth to their humor. For instance, a puppet who is perpetually clumsy may have a backstory that explains their lack of coordination, making their mishaps even funnier. Puppeteers should take the time to develop their characters' histories, as this can enhance the audience's connection to the humor.

5. Experimentation and Adaptation

Creating comedic characters is an iterative process. Puppeteers should be open to experimentation, trying out different traits, voices, and interactions to see what resonates with audiences. Feedback from performances can guide adjustments and refinements, allowing characters to evolve into their most humorous selves. Embracing the fluidity of character development can lead to delightful surprises and unexpected comedic moments.

Chapter 12: Emotional Depth in Characters

Building Empathy

The essence of puppetry lies not merely in the manipulation of inanimate objects but in the profound connection that can be forged between the puppeteer, the puppet, and the audience. To create characters that resonate deeply, one must first understand the concept of empathy. Empathy is the ability to understand and share the feelings of another, and it is this emotional bridge that allows audiences to connect with puppet characters on a personal level.

When designing a puppet character, consider their emotional landscape. What experiences have shaped them? What fears and desires drive their actions? By delving into these questions, puppeteers can craft characters that feel authentic and relatable. For instance, a puppet that has faced adversity may evoke sympathy, while one that embodies joy and resilience can inspire hope.

To build empathy, it is essential to incorporate universal themes that resonate across cultures and generations. Love, loss, friendship, and betrayal are emotions that everyone can relate to, regardless of their background. By embedding these themes into the character's journey, puppeteers can create a narrative that transcends the boundaries of language and culture.

Moreover, the physicality of the puppet plays a significant role in conveying emotion. The way a puppet moves, its facial expressions, and even the materials used in its construction can all contribute to the audience's emotional response. A puppet with soft, rounded features may evoke warmth and comfort, while sharp angles and rigid movements might suggest tension or conflict.

Incorporating subtle gestures and expressions can further enhance the emotional depth of a character. A slight tilt of the head, a gentle wave of the hand, or a sudden pause can communicate a wealth of feelings without the need for words. This non-verbal communication is crucial in puppetry, as it allows the audience to engage with the character on a deeper emotional level.

Ultimately, building empathy in puppet characters requires a delicate balance of storytelling, physicality, and emotional authenticity. By investing time in understanding the character's emotional journey, puppeteers can create memorable and impactful experiences for their audiences.

Emotional Arcs

Every compelling story is driven by the emotional arcs of its characters. An emotional arc refers to the transformation that a character undergoes throughout the narrative, shaped by their experiences, challenges, and relationships. In puppetry, crafting a well-defined emotional arc is essential for creating characters that resonate with audiences.

To begin, consider the character's starting point. What are their initial emotions, beliefs, and motivations? This foundation sets the stage for the character's journey. For example, a puppet that begins as a timid and insecure figure may face challenges that force them to confront their fears and ultimately emerge as a confident leader.

As the story unfolds, the character should encounter obstacles that challenge their beliefs and force them to grow. These challenges can take various forms, such as external conflicts with other characters or internal struggles with self-doubt. The key is to ensure that these obstacles are meaningful and relevant to the character's emotional journey.

The climax of the story often serves as a turning point for the character, where they must confront their greatest fears or make a significant decision. This moment of crisis is crucial, as it allows the audience to witness the character's growth and transformation. For instance, a puppet that has been running away from their problems may finally choose to face them head-on, demonstrating courage and resilience.

Following the climax, the resolution of the story should reflect the character's emotional growth. How have they changed? What lessons have they learned? This resolution provides closure for both the character and the audience, allowing them to reflect on the journey they have shared.

To illustrate the concept of emotional arcs, consider the following table that outlines a basic structure for developing a character's emotional journey:

Stage	Description	Example
1. Introduction	Establish the character's initial emotional state and background.	A shy puppet who struggles to make friends.
2. Inciting Incident	A challenge or event that disrupts the character's status quo.	The puppet is invited to a party but fears rejection.
3. Rising Action	The character faces obstacles that test their beliefs and emotions.	The puppet encounters a bully at the party.
4. Climax	The turning point where the character confronts their greatest challenge.	The puppet stands up to the bully, gaining confidence.
5. Falling Action	The aftermath of the climax, showing the character's growth.	The puppet makes new friends and feels accepted.
6. Resolution	The character's emotional state at the end of the story, reflecting their journey.	The puppet is now confident and happy, having learned the value of friendship.

By following this structure, puppeteers can create emotionally rich characters that engage audiences and leave a lasting impression. The emotional arc not only enhances the character's depth but also enriches the overall narrative, making it more compelling and relatable.

Relatable Struggles

At the heart of every memorable puppet character lies a struggle that resonates with the audience. Relatable struggles are the challenges and conflicts that characters face, which reflect the human experience. By incorporating these struggles into puppet narratives, puppeteers can create characters that evoke empathy and connection.

One of the most effective ways to create relatable struggles is to draw from real-life experiences. Consider the challenges that individuals face in their daily lives—fear of failure, the desire for acceptance, the quest for identity, and the struggle to overcome adversity. By weaving these themes into the character's journey, puppeteers can create narratives that resonate with audiences on a personal level.

For instance, a puppet character grappling with self-doubt may mirror the insecurities that many individuals face in their own lives. By portraying this struggle authentically, the puppeteer can foster a sense of connection with the audience, allowing them to see themselves in the character's journey.

Moreover, the resolution of these struggles is equally important. Characters that overcome their challenges often inspire hope and resilience in the audience. For example, a puppet that learns to embrace their uniqueness and celebrate their differences can serve as a powerful reminder of the importance of self-acceptance.

Incorporating humor into relatable struggles can also enhance the emotional depth of the character. Laughter can serve as a coping mechanism, allowing audiences to engage with difficult themes in a lighthearted manner. A puppet that navigates the ups and downs of life with a sense of humor can create a joyful experience while still addressing serious issues.

To further illustrate the concept of relatable struggles, consider the following table that highlights common struggles and their potential resolutions:

Struggle	Description	Potential Resolution
Fear of Failure	The character is afraid to take risks due to past failures.	They learn that failure is a part of growth and embrace new challenges.
Desire for Acceptance	The character feels out of place and longs for friendship.	They discover that true friends appreciate them for who they are.
Identity Crisis	The character struggles to understand their place in the world.	They embark on a journey of self-discovery and find their true passion.
Overcoming Adversity	The character faces significant challenges that test their resilience.	They learn to persevere and emerge stronger from their experiences.

By incorporating relatable struggles into puppet narratives, puppeteers can create characters that resonate with audiences and evoke genuine emotional responses. These struggles not only enhance the depth of the character but also foster a sense of connection and understanding between the puppeteer and the audience.

Chapter 13: Cultural Influences on Character Creation

Cultural Sensitivity

Cultural sensitivity is a vital aspect of character creation in puppetry. As puppeteers, we have the unique opportunity to bring diverse stories and characters to life, but with this privilege comes the responsibility to approach cultural representation with care and respect. The world is a tapestry of cultures, each with its own rich history, traditions, and values. When creating puppet characters that draw from these cultures, it is essential to engage in thoughtful research and reflection. Understanding the nuances of a culture is paramount. This involves delving into its language, customs, and social norms. A character that embodies a specific cultural background should reflect the authenticity of that culture, rather than relying on stereotypes or superficial traits. For instance, a puppet representing a Native American character should not only wear traditional attire but also embody the values and beliefs of the community it represents. This requires a deep understanding of the culture's history, struggles, and triumphs. Moreover, it is crucial to consider the voices behind the characters. Collaborating with individuals from the culture being represented can provide invaluable insights and perspectives. This collaboration fosters a more genuine portrayal and helps avoid misrepresentation. Engaging with cultural consultants or community members can enrich the character's development and ensure that it resonates with authenticity. In addition to collaboration, self-reflection is essential. Puppeteers must examine their own biases and assumptions. It is important to recognize that our perspectives are shaped by our own cultural backgrounds, and this can influence how we create characters. By acknowledging our limitations and being open to learning, we can create more nuanced and respectful representations. Ultimately, cultural sensitivity in puppetry is about honoring the stories and experiences of diverse communities. It is an invitation to celebrate the richness of human experience while fostering understanding and empathy. By approaching character creation with cultural sensitivity, puppeteers can create characters that not only entertain but also educate and inspire.

Incorporating Traditions

Incorporating traditions into puppet character creation adds depth and richness to the storytelling experience. Every culture has its own unique traditions, rituals, and folklore that can serve as a wellspring of inspiration for character development. By weaving these elements into our puppetry, we can create characters that resonate with audiences on a profound level. One way to incorporate traditions is through the use of traditional storytelling techniques. Many cultures have their own methods of storytelling, whether through oral traditions, dance, or music. By integrating these techniques into puppet performances, we can create a more immersive experience for the audience. For example, a puppet show that incorporates traditional African drumming or Native American storytelling can transport viewers into the heart of the culture being represented. Additionally, traditional art forms can inspire character design. The vibrant colors, patterns, and motifs found in traditional textiles, pottery, and crafts can inform the visual aesthetics of puppet characters. For instance, a puppet inspired by Japanese culture might feature intricate kimono patterns, while a character from Indigenous cultures might showcase designs that reflect the natural world. By paying homage to these artistic traditions, puppeteers can create visually stunning characters that honor their cultural roots. Furthermore, rituals and ceremonies can provide a framework for character development. Many cultures have specific rites of passage or celebrations that can serve as pivotal moments in a puppet character's journey. For example, a puppet character might undergo a transformation during a coming-of-age ceremony, symbolizing growth and change. By incorporating these traditions into the narrative, puppeteers can create characters that embody the values and beliefs of their cultures. It is also essential to consider the role of community in traditions. Many cultural practices are communal in nature, emphasizing the importance of relationships and connections. Puppeteers can reflect this by creating ensemble casts of characters that represent various aspects of a community. This not only enriches the storytelling but also highlights the interconnectedness of individuals within a culture. Incorporating traditions into puppet character creation is a celebration of cultural heritage. It invites audiences to engage with the stories and practices that shape our world, fostering a deeper appreciation for the diversity of human experience. By honoring these traditions, puppeteers can create characters that resonate with authenticity and meaning.

Diverse Characters

Diversity in character creation is essential for reflecting the multifaceted nature of our world. Puppetry offers a unique platform to showcase a wide range of characters, each with their own stories, backgrounds, and experiences. By embracing diversity, puppeteers can create characters that resonate with audiences from various cultural backgrounds, fostering inclusivity and understanding. When developing diverse characters, it is important to move beyond tokenism. Each character should be fully realized, with their own distinct personality, motivations, and arcs. This requires a commitment to depth and complexity. For instance, a puppet character representing a Hispanic individual should not only reflect cultural traits but also embody the richness of their personal experiences, dreams, and challenges. By creating well-rounded characters, puppeteers can challenge stereotypes and promote empathy. Moreover, diverse characters can serve as powerful role models for audiences. Representation matters, and seeing characters that reflect different backgrounds can inspire individuals to embrace their own identities. For example, a puppet character who navigates the challenges of being a first-generation immigrant can resonate with children and adults alike, fostering a sense of connection and understanding. These characters can empower audiences to celebrate their own stories and experiences. In addition to cultural diversity, it is essential to consider other dimensions of diversity, such as gender, age, ability, and socioeconomic status. Each of these aspects contributes to the richness of human experience and can inform character development. A puppet character who is a senior citizen, for instance, can offer wisdom and perspective, while a character with a disability can challenge perceptions and promote inclusivity. Collaboration with diverse voices is crucial in this process. Engaging with individuals from various backgrounds can provide valuable insights and perspectives that enhance character development. This collaboration can take many forms, from consulting with cultural experts to involving community members in the creative process. By amplifying diverse voices, puppeteers can create characters that resonate authentically with their intended audiences. Ultimately, the goal of creating diverse characters is to foster understanding and connection. Puppetry has the power to transcend cultural boundaries, allowing audiences to engage with stories that reflect the richness of human experience. By embracing diversity in character creation, puppeteers can create a more inclusive and vibrant storytelling landscape that resonates with audiences of all backgrounds.

Chapter 14: Collaborating with Other Artists

Collaboration is the lifeblood of creativity, particularly in the realm of puppetry, where the fusion of various artistic disciplines can lead to the birth of truly extraordinary characters and performances. The art of puppetry is not merely a solitary endeavor; it thrives on the synergy that emerges when writers, designers, and performers come together, each contributing their unique skills and perspectives. This chapter delves into the intricacies of collaboration, exploring how to effectively work with other artists to enhance character creation and elevate the overall puppetry experience.

Working with Writers, Designers, and Performers

In the world of puppetry, the collaborative process begins with the writers, who lay the groundwork for the narrative that will guide the puppet characters. A well-crafted script serves as the backbone of any puppet show, providing context, dialogue, and emotional arcs that breathe life into the characters. When collaborating with writers, it is essential to engage in open dialogue, sharing ideas and visions for the characters. This exchange can lead to a richer narrative, as writers may draw inspiration from the unique qualities of the puppets themselves. Consider the character of a whimsical, mischievous puppet. A writer might envision a storyline that highlights the puppet's playful nature, incorporating clever dialogue and humorous situations. However, the puppet creator can provide valuable insights into the puppet's physicality and movement, suggesting how the character's design can influence the narrative. For instance, if the puppet has oversized hands, the writer might craft scenes that emphasize the puppet's clumsiness, creating comedic moments that resonate with the audience. In addition to writers, designers play a crucial role in the collaborative process. The visual aspect of puppetry is paramount, as it sets the tone and atmosphere for the performance. Designers are responsible for creating the aesthetic elements that complement the characters, including costumes, props, and set design.

When working with designers, it is vital to communicate the essence of each character, discussing their personality traits, backstory, and emotional depth. This collaboration allows designers to create costumes that not only enhance the puppet's appearance but also reflect their character's journey. For example, a puppet character that embodies wisdom and age might be adorned with flowing robes and intricate accessories that signify their experience. In contrast, a youthful, energetic puppet may wear vibrant colors and playful patterns that capture their exuberance. By collaborating closely with designers, puppet creators can ensure that the visual elements align harmoniously with the character's narrative, creating a cohesive and immersive experience for the audience. Performers, too, are integral to the collaborative process. The way a puppet is brought to life hinges on the skill and creativity of the performer. When working with performers, it is essential to foster an environment of trust and experimentation. Each performer brings their unique interpretation to the character, and this individuality can lead to unexpected and delightful outcomes. Encouraging performers to explore different vocalizations, movements, and expressions can result in a richer portrayal of the puppet character. Consider a puppet that is meant to convey a sense of joy and playfulness. A performer might experiment with various voice inflections, using a high-pitched tone to emphasize the character's excitement. Additionally, the performer may incorporate exaggerated movements, such as bouncing or twirling, to enhance the character's lively spirit. By allowing performers the freedom to explore their interpretations, puppet creators can discover new dimensions of their characters that may not have been initially envisioned.

Collaboration also extends beyond the immediate team of writers, designers, and performers. Engaging with other artists, such as musicians and sound designers, can further enrich the puppetry experience. Music and sound play a pivotal role in setting the mood and enhancing the emotional impact of a performance. When collaborating with musicians, it is essential to discuss the character's emotional journey and the desired atmosphere for each scene. This collaboration can lead to the creation of original compositions that resonate with the audience and elevate the overall storytelling. For instance, a puppet character experiencing a moment of triumph may be accompanied by a triumphant musical score, while a scene of introspection might feature softer, more contemplative melodies. By working closely with musicians, puppet creators can ensure that the auditory elements align seamlessly with the visual and narrative components, creating a holistic experience for the audience. In addition to the artistic aspects, collaboration in puppetry also involves logistical considerations. Coordinating schedules, managing resources, and ensuring effective communication are essential components of a successful collaborative process. Establishing clear roles and responsibilities within the team can help streamline the workflow and prevent misunderstandings. Regular meetings and check-ins can facilitate open communication, allowing team members to share updates, address challenges, and celebrate successes. Moreover, fostering a culture of respect and appreciation within the collaborative team is crucial. Each artist brings their unique talents and perspectives to the table, and recognizing the value of each contribution can strengthen the collaborative bond. Celebrating milestones, whether big or small, can create a positive atmosphere that encourages creativity and innovation. As the collaborative process unfolds, it is important to remain flexible and open to new ideas. The beauty of collaboration lies in the unexpected connections and discoveries that can arise when artists come together. Embracing spontaneity and allowing room for experimentation can lead to innovative character creations that captivate audiences in ways that may not have been initially anticipated.

In conclusion, collaboration is an essential aspect of the art of puppetry, enriching the character creation process and enhancing the overall performance. By working closely with writers, designers, performers, and other artists, puppet creators can develop multifaceted characters that resonate with audiences on a deeper level. The synergy that emerges from collaboration not only elevates the puppetry experience but also fosters a sense of community among artists, creating a vibrant tapestry of creativity that celebrates the art of puppetry in all its forms.

Chapter 15: The Importance of Rehearsal

Rehearsal is the sacred ground where the alchemy of puppetry transforms mere ideas into vibrant, breathing characters. It is a space where the puppeteer and the puppet engage in a dance of creativity, allowing the essence of the character to emerge fully. This chapter delves into the multifaceted nature of rehearsal, exploring its significance in practicing characterization, the nuances of timing and rhythm, and the invaluable role of feedback loops.

Practicing Characterization

Rehearsal is not merely a mechanical process of running through lines or movements; it is an immersive experience that allows puppeteers to delve deep into the psyche of their characters. Practicing characterization during rehearsal involves embodying the puppet, understanding its motivations, and exploring its emotional landscape. To begin, it is essential to approach each rehearsal with an open mind and a willingness to experiment. The puppeteer must step into the shoes of the character, allowing their own inhibitions to dissolve. This process often involves improvisation, where the puppeteer can explore different facets of the character's personality. For instance, if a character is known for being mischievous, the puppeteer might experiment with various ways to express that trait through movement and voice. In this exploration, the puppeteer should pay attention to the physicality of the puppet. How does the puppet's design influence its movements? A puppet with long limbs may lend itself to graceful, sweeping gestures, while a stocky puppet might convey strength through more grounded movements. By understanding the physical attributes of the puppet, the puppeteer can enhance the characterization, making it more authentic and relatable. Moreover, practicing characterization involves vocal experimentation. The voice of a puppet is a critical component of its identity. During rehearsal, the puppeteer should explore different vocal qualities, pitches, and speech patterns. For example, a character that is wise and elderly may benefit from a slow, deliberate speech pattern, while a youthful character might speak rapidly and with enthusiasm. This vocal exploration not only adds depth to the character but also helps the puppeteer to connect emotionally with the puppet. Another vital aspect of practicing characterization is the development of relationships between characters. Rehearsals provide an opportunity to explore the dynamics between different puppets. How does one character react to another? What is the nature of their relationship? By rehearsing these interactions, the puppeteer can create a more cohesive and engaging narrative. In addition to individual character work, group rehearsals are invaluable. They allow puppeteers to witness how their characters interact with others, providing insights into the overall story arc. The synergy that develops in group rehearsals can lead to unexpected discoveries, enriching the performance and enhancing the audience's experience. Ultimately, practicing characterization during rehearsal is about finding the heart of the character. It is a journey of discovery, where the puppeteer learns to listen to the puppet and respond to its unique voice. This process not only strengthens the character but also fosters a deeper connection between the puppeteer and the puppet, resulting in a more compelling performance.

Timing and Rhythm

Timing and rhythm are the lifeblood of puppetry, infusing performances with energy and engagement. In rehearsal, the exploration of timing and rhythm is essential for creating a captivating experience for the audience. The interplay of these elements can elevate a performance from ordinary to extraordinary, transforming simple movements into a symphony of expression. At the heart of timing is the concept of pacing. Pacing refers to the speed at which actions and dialogue unfold. During rehearsal, puppeteers must experiment with different tempos to find the most effective pacing for their characters and scenes. A scene filled with tension may benefit from a slower pace, allowing the audience to absorb the gravity of the moment. Conversely, a comedic scene may thrive on rapid-fire exchanges and quick movements, generating laughter and excitement. Rhythm, on the other hand, encompasses the patterns of movement and sound that create a sense of flow within the performance. It is the heartbeat of the puppetry, guiding the audience through the narrative. In rehearsal, puppeteers should pay attention to the rhythm of their movements, ensuring that they align with the emotional beats of the story. For instance, a character experiencing joy may move in a lively, bouncy rhythm, while a character in despair may exhibit a heavy, dragging rhythm. To master timing and rhythm, puppeteers can incorporate exercises that focus on these elements. One effective exercise involves pairing movements with music. By selecting a piece of music that resonates with the character or scene, puppeteers can explore how the rhythm of the music influences their movements. This exercise not only enhances the puppeteer's understanding of timing but also allows them to discover new ways to express their character's emotions. Another valuable technique is to practice with a metronome. This tool can help puppeteers develop a sense of timing, ensuring that their movements and dialogue are synchronized. By setting a specific tempo, puppeteers can experiment with different rhythms, discovering what feels most natural for their character. This practice can be particularly beneficial for comedic timing, where precise delivery is crucial for eliciting laughter. In addition to individual practice, group rehearsals provide an opportunity to refine timing and rhythm collaboratively. When multiple puppeteers are involved, it becomes essential to establish a shared sense of timing. This can be achieved through exercises that emphasize ensemble work, such as group improvisation or synchronized movements. By working together, puppeteers can create a cohesive rhythm that enhances the overall performance. The importance of timing and rhythm extends beyond the physical movements of the puppets; it also encompasses the delivery of dialogue. The way lines are spoken can significantly impact the audience's perception of the characters and the story. During rehearsal, puppeteers should experiment with different inflections, pauses, and emphases to find the most effective delivery for their lines. This exploration can lead to moments of surprise, humor, or poignancy, enriching the performance. Ultimately, the mastery of timing and rhythm is a continuous journey. Rehearsals provide the space for puppeteers to refine these skills, allowing them to create performances that resonate with audiences on a profound level. By embracing the nuances of timing and rhythm, puppeteers can elevate their characters, transforming them into dynamic, memorable figures that leave a lasting impression.

Feedback Loops

Feedback loops are an integral part of the rehearsal process, serving as a vital mechanism for growth and improvement. In the world of puppetry, feedback can come from various sources, including fellow puppeteers, directors, and even the audience. Embracing feedback is essential for refining performances and enhancing character development. During rehearsals, it is crucial to create an environment where feedback is welcomed and encouraged. This atmosphere fosters collaboration and allows puppeteers to feel safe in exploring their characters without fear of judgment. One effective way to establish this environment is through structured feedback sessions. After a rehearsal, the team can gather to discuss what worked well and what could be improved. This collaborative approach not only strengthens the bond between puppeteers but also leads to richer performances. When receiving feedback, it is essential for puppeteers to approach it with an open mind. Constructive criticism can provide valuable insights into aspects of the performance that may need refinement. For instance, a fellow puppeteer may notice that a character's movements lack clarity or that the emotional beats are not landing as intended. By being receptive to this feedback, puppeteers can make adjustments that enhance the overall impact of their performance. In addition to peer feedback, directors play a crucial role in guiding the rehearsal process. Their outside perspective can illuminate areas for improvement that puppeteers may overlook. Directors often have a broader vision for the production, and their feedback can help puppeteers align their performances with the overall narrative. Regular check-ins with the director during rehearsal can ensure that the character development remains consistent with the story's arc. Audience feedback is another invaluable resource for puppeteers. While rehearsals are often closed to the public, inviting a small audience for a preview performance can provide insights into how the characters resonate with viewers. Observing audience reactions can reveal which moments land effectively and which may need further refinement. This feedback loop between the puppeteer and the audience is essential for creating a performance that connects on an emotional level. Moreover, self-reflection is a powerful tool in the feedback process. After each rehearsal, puppeteers should take time to assess their own performances. What felt right? What felt off? This introspection allows puppeteers to identify patterns in their work and make conscious choices moving forward. Keeping a rehearsal journal can be beneficial, as it provides a space to document thoughts, observations, and areas for improvement. Incorporating feedback loops into the rehearsal process is not just about making adjustments; it is also about celebrating successes. Acknowledging what works well reinforces positive behaviors and encourages puppeteers to continue exploring those elements. Celebrating small victories, whether it's nailing a comedic timing or successfully conveying a character's emotional arc, fosters a sense of accomplishment and motivation. Ultimately, feedback loops are a dynamic and ongoing process that enriches the rehearsal experience. By embracing feedback from peers, directors, and audiences, puppeteers can refine their performances and deepen their understanding of character development. This iterative process not only enhances the quality of the performance but also nurtures the growth of the puppeteer as an artist, leading to a more profound connection with their characters and the audience.

Chapter 16: Creating Dynamic Relationships

Creating dynamic relationships between puppet characters is an essential aspect of puppetry that breathes life into performances. The interactions, conflicts, and resolutions that unfold on stage not only engage the audience but also develop the characters in profound ways. This chapter delves into the intricacies of character interactions, the nature of conflict and resolution, and the dynamics that arise within groups of puppets.

Character Interactions

At the heart of any compelling puppet show lies the interactions between characters. These exchanges can range from light-hearted banter to deep emotional connections, and they serve as the foundation for storytelling. Understanding how to craft these interactions is crucial for any puppeteer aiming to create memorable characters.

Establishing Relationships

The first step in creating dynamic relationships is to establish the nature of the connection between characters. Are they friends, rivals, family members, or strangers? Each type of relationship brings its own set of dynamics and expectations. For instance, a friendship may be characterized by support and camaraderie, while a rivalry could be filled with tension and competition.

To illustrate this, consider the following table that outlines different relationship types and their characteristics:

Relationship Type	Characteristics
Friendship	Supportive, Trusting, Fun
Rivalry	Competitive, Tense, Challenging
Family	Complex, Emotional, Loyal
Strangers	Curious, Awkward, Uncertain

By defining the nature of the relationships, puppeteers can create a framework for how characters will interact with one another. This framework serves as a guide for dialogue, movement, and emotional expression.

Dialogue and Communication Styles

Once the relationships are established, the next step is to develop the dialogue and communication styles of the characters. Each character should have a unique voice that reflects their personality and relationship with others. For example, a confident character may speak assertively, while a shy character may use softer tones and hesitant phrases.

Consider the following examples of dialogue styles based on character types:

Character Type	Dialogue Style
Confident Leader	Direct, Commanding, Inspirational
Witty Sidekick	Humorous, Sarcastic, Playful
Timid Character	Soft, Hesitant, Insecure
Wise Mentor	Thoughtful, Reflective, Encouraging

By varying dialogue styles, puppeteers can enhance the richness of character interactions and make them more engaging for the audience.

Physical Interactions

In addition to verbal communication, physical interactions play a significant role in character relationships. The way puppets move and react to one another can convey emotions and intentions that words alone cannot express. For instance, a character might lean in closer to show interest or take a step back to indicate discomfort.

Puppeteers should consider the following aspects when crafting physical interactions:

1. Proximity: The distance between characters can convey intimacy or tension. Characters who are close together may share secrets or express affection, while those who are farther apart may be in conflict or disagreement.

2. Gestures: Specific gestures can enhance communication. A wave, a shrug, or a pointed finger can all add layers of meaning to interactions.

3. Facial Expressions: Even though puppets may have limited facial features, subtle changes in expression can convey a wide range of emotions. A raised eyebrow or a frown can indicate surprise or disapproval.

By thoughtfully integrating these elements, puppeteers can create interactions that resonate with the audience and deepen their understanding of the characters.

Conflict and Resolution

Conflict is an inherent part of storytelling, and it serves as a catalyst for character development. In puppetry, conflicts can arise from misunderstandings, differing goals, or external pressures. The resolution of these conflicts is equally important, as it provides closure and growth for the characters involved.

Types of Conflict

Understanding the different types of conflict can help puppeteers create compelling narratives. Here are some common types of conflict that can be explored in puppet shows:

Type of Conflict	Description
Character vs. Character	Direct confrontation between two characters with opposing goals.
Character vs. Self	Internal struggle within a character, often involving doubts or fears.
Character vs. Society	Conflict arising from societal norms or expectations that challenge a character.

Type of Conflict	Description
Character vs. Nature	Struggles against natural forces or circumstances beyond a character's control.

Each type of conflict offers unique opportunities for character growth and audience engagement. By selecting the appropriate conflict for the story, puppeteers can create tension that captivates viewers.

Building Tension

Tension is a critical component of conflict, and it can be built through various techniques. Here are some strategies to create tension in puppet performances:

1. Raising Stakes: As the conflict unfolds, increasing the stakes can heighten tension. This could involve introducing new challenges or consequences that affect the characters' goals.

2. Pacing: The rhythm of the performance can influence tension. Slowing down moments of conflict can create suspense, while quickening the pace can lead to chaotic resolutions.

3. Cliffhangers: Ending scenes on a cliffhanger can leave the audience eager to see how the conflict will be resolved. This technique encourages engagement and anticipation.

By employing these strategies, puppeteers can create a gripping narrative that keeps the audience invested in the outcome.

Resolution and Growth

The resolution of conflict is a pivotal moment in any story, as it allows characters to evolve and learn from their experiences. In puppetry, resolutions can take many forms, from reconciliation to personal growth.

Consider the following approaches to resolution:

1. Reconciliation: Characters may come to an understanding or forgiveness, leading to a renewed relationship. This can be a powerful moment that emphasizes the importance of empathy and communication.

2. Personal Growth: Sometimes, characters emerge from conflict with newfound wisdom or strength. This growth can be portrayed through changes in behavior, attitude, or perspective.

3. Consequences: Not all resolutions are positive. Characters may face consequences for their actions, leading to a more somber or reflective ending. This can provoke thought and discussion among the audience.

By thoughtfully crafting resolutions, puppeteers can leave a lasting impact on their viewers, encouraging them to reflect on the themes presented in the performance.

Group Dynamics

In many puppet performances, characters exist within a group dynamic that influences their interactions and relationships. Understanding how to navigate these dynamics is essential for creating a cohesive and engaging performance.

Character Roles within Groups

Each character in a group often assumes a specific role that contributes to the overall dynamic. These roles can include:

Character Role	Description
Leader	Guides the group and makes decisions.
Peacemaker	Attempts to resolve conflicts and maintain harmony.
Rebel	Challenges authority and pushes boundaries.
Supporter	Provides encouragement and assistance to others.

By defining these roles, puppeteers can create a rich tapestry of interactions that reflect the complexities of group dynamics.

Group Interactions

Interactions within groups can be both collaborative and competitive. Characters may work together towards a common goal or find themselves at odds with one another. The interplay of these dynamics can lead to engaging storytelling.

1. Collaboration: Characters may join forces to overcome obstacles, showcasing teamwork and camaraderie. This can be depicted through synchronized movements, shared dialogue, and collective problem-solving.

2. Competition: Rivalries within the group can create tension and excitement. Characters may vie for attention, resources, or recognition, leading to humorous or dramatic exchanges.

3. Conflict Resolution: Groups often face challenges that require negotiation and compromise. Characters must navigate their differences to find common ground, highlighting the importance of communication and understanding.

By exploring these interactions, puppeteers can create a vibrant and dynamic performance that resonates with audiences.

Impact of Group Dynamics on Character Development

The dynamics within a group can significantly influence character development. As characters interact with one another, they may experience growth, change, or reinforcement of their existing traits.

1. Influence of Peers: Characters may be swayed by the opinions and actions of their peers, leading to shifts in behavior or perspective. This can be particularly impactful in group settings where conformity or rebellion is at play.

2. Support Systems: Positive group dynamics can foster personal growth and resilience. Characters who feel supported by their peers may be more willing to take

risks and explore new facets of their personalities.

3. Conflict as a Catalyst: Conflicts within the group can serve as catalysts for change. Characters may confront their fears, challenge their beliefs, or develop new skills as they navigate the complexities of group interactions.

By recognizing the impact of group dynamics, puppeteers can create multi-dimensional characters that resonate with audiences on a deeper level.

Chapter 17: The Role of Music and Sound

Choosing Soundscapes

The world of puppetry is a vibrant tapestry woven from various threads of creativity, and soundscapes play a pivotal role in enriching this artistic expression. Soundscapes are not merely background noise; they are the auditory landscapes that envelop the audience, enhancing the emotional resonance of the performance. When selecting soundscapes, one must consider the thematic elements of the puppet show, the characters involved, and the overall atmosphere one wishes to create. To begin with, it is essential to identify the mood of the performance. Is it whimsical and light-hearted, or dark and mysterious? The choice of soundscape should reflect this mood. For instance, a playful puppet show featuring mischievous characters might benefit from lively, upbeat music accompanied by sounds of laughter and playful chatter. In contrast, a more serious narrative may require a somber soundscape, perhaps incorporating ambient sounds like rustling leaves or distant thunder to evoke a sense of tension or foreboding. Furthermore, the cultural context of the puppet characters can greatly influence the soundscapes chosen. Different cultures have distinct musical traditions and sound patterns that can add authenticity to the performance. For example, if the puppets are inspired by a specific cultural background, incorporating traditional instruments or folk melodies can create a deeper connection with the audience. This not only enriches the viewing experience but also pays homage to the cultural roots of the characters being portrayed. In addition to cultural considerations, the physical setting of the performance should guide soundscape choices. A puppet show set in a bustling market might feature a cacophony of sounds—vendors calling out, children laughing, and the distant sound of music. Conversely, a scene set in a tranquil forest could be accompanied by the gentle sounds of birds chirping and leaves rustling in the wind. By aligning the soundscape with the visual elements of the performance, puppeteers can create a cohesive and immersive experience for the audience. Moreover, the use of silence can be just as powerful as sound. Strategic pauses in the auditory landscape can heighten tension, draw attention to a pivotal moment, or allow the audience to reflect on what they have just witnessed. Silence can serve as a canvas upon which the subsequent sounds can paint a more vivid picture, making the eventual return of music or sound all the more impactful. Ultimately, the selection of soundscapes is an art form in itself, requiring careful consideration and creativity. It is an opportunity for puppeteers to explore the auditory dimensions of their characters and narratives, crafting an experience that resonates deeply with the audience. By thoughtfully choosing soundscapes, puppeteers can elevate their performances, transforming them into multi-sensory journeys that linger in the hearts and minds of viewers long after the curtain falls.

Musical Themes

Music is the heartbeat of any performance, and in the realm of puppetry, it serves as a powerful tool for character development and storytelling. The incorporation of musical themes can imbue puppet characters with distinct identities, allowing audiences to connect with them on a deeper emotional level. Each character can have its own musical motif, a unique melody that encapsulates its essence and journey throughout the performance. When crafting musical themes for puppet characters, it is essential to consider their personalities, motivations, and arcs. A brave and adventurous puppet might be accompanied by a bold, triumphant theme, characterized by strong brass and percussion, evoking a sense of courage and determination. In contrast, a timid and shy character may have a softer, more delicate melody, perhaps featuring strings or woodwinds that convey a sense of vulnerability and introspection. The use of recurring musical motifs can also enhance the narrative structure of the puppet show. Just as a novel employs themes to unify its chapters, a puppet performance can weave musical motifs throughout its scenes, creating a sense of continuity and cohesion. When a character reappears, their theme can resurface, reminding the audience of their journey and emotional state. This technique not only reinforces character development but also allows the audience to engage with the story on a more profound level. Moreover, the interplay between musical themes and character interactions can add layers of complexity to the performance. When two characters share a scene, their themes can intertwine, creating a musical dialogue that reflects their relationship. For instance, a playful rivalry between two puppets might be expressed through contrasting musical motifs that play off each other, highlighting their dynamic and adding an element of humor to the performance. Alternatively, a moment of reconciliation could be underscored by a harmonious blending of their themes, symbolizing their growth and understanding. In addition to character themes, the overall musical score should complement the pacing and structure of the performance. Just as a skilled conductor guides an orchestra, the music should ebb and flow with the action on stage, enhancing moments of tension, joy, and reflection. A well-timed crescendo can elevate a climactic scene, while a gentle lullaby can provide a moment of respite, allowing the audience to absorb the emotional weight of the narrative. Furthermore, the choice of instruments can significantly influence the character of the music. Traditional instruments can evoke a sense of nostalgia or cultural authenticity, while modern electronic sounds can create a contemporary feel. The fusion of different musical styles can also reflect the diversity of the characters and their experiences, enriching the overall tapestry of the performance. Ultimately, the creation of musical themes is a collaborative process that involves not only the puppeteer but also composers, musicians, and sound designers. By working together, they can craft a musical landscape that resonates with the audience, elevating the puppetry experience to new heights. Through the careful selection and integration of musical themes, puppeteers can breathe life into their characters, transforming them into memorable figures that linger in the hearts and minds of viewers.

Enhancing Character Presence

The presence of a puppet character is not solely defined by its physical appearance or movements; it is also significantly influenced by the auditory elements that accompany it. Sound and music play a crucial role in enhancing character presence, allowing puppeteers to create a more immersive and engaging experience for the audience. By thoughtfully integrating sound into the performance, puppeteers can elevate their characters from mere objects to vibrant, dynamic personalities. One of the most effective ways to enhance character presence is through the use of voice. The voice of a puppet can convey a wealth of information about its personality, background, and emotional state. A character's voice should be distinct and recognizable, allowing the audience to connect with it on a personal level. Puppeteers can experiment with pitch, tone, and accent to create unique vocal identities for their characters. A gruff, deep voice might suggest strength and authority, while a high-pitched, squeaky voice could evoke playfulness and innocence. In addition to voice, the use of sound effects can significantly enhance character presence. Sound effects can be employed to emphasize specific actions or emotions, adding an extra layer of depth to the performance. For example, the sound of footsteps can accompany a character's entrance, creating a sense of anticipation and drawing the audience's attention. Similarly, the sound of a heartbeat can heighten tension during a dramatic moment, allowing the audience to feel the character's anxiety or fear. Moreover, the integration of music can further amplify character presence. As previously discussed, musical themes can encapsulate a character's essence, but they can also serve to underscore key moments in the performance. A character's entrance might be accompanied by a triumphant fanfare, while a moment of vulnerability could be underscored by a soft, melancholic melody. By aligning the music with the character's emotional journey, puppeteers can create a more profound connection between the audience and the characters on stage. The timing of sound and music is also crucial in enhancing character presence. A well-timed sound effect or musical cue can draw the audience's attention to a specific moment, allowing them to fully engage with the character's experience. For instance, a sudden burst of music can heighten the impact of a comedic moment, while a gradual fade-out can create a sense of reflection and introspection. By mastering the timing of sound and music, puppeteers can guide the audience's emotional responses and deepen their engagement with the performance. Furthermore, the use of silence can be a powerful tool in enhancing character presence. Strategic pauses in the auditory landscape can create moments of tension, allowing the audience to absorb the weight of a character's actions or decisions. Silence can serve as a canvas upon which the subsequent sounds can paint a more vivid picture, making the eventual return of music or sound all the more impactful. By embracing silence as a part of the auditory experience, puppeteers can create a more nuanced and layered performance.

Chapter 18: Designing Costumes for Puppets

Costumes are the vibrant fabric of a puppet's identity, weaving together the threads of personality, story, and emotion. They serve not only as a visual representation of the character but also as an essential tool for conveying the nuances of performance. In this chapter, we will explore the intricacies of designing costumes for puppets, delving into the basics of costume design, the selection of fabrics, and the art of accessorizing characters.

Costume Basics

At the heart of puppet costume design lies an understanding of the character itself. Each puppet, whether a whimsical creature or a serious figure, demands a costume that reflects its essence. The first step in this creative journey is to analyze the character's traits, backstory, and role within the narrative.

When embarking on the design process, consider the following elements:

1. Character Identity

The costume must resonate with the character's identity. Is your puppet a mischievous trickster or a wise sage? The colors, patterns, and styles you choose should align with the character's personality. For instance, bright, bold colors may suit a lively, energetic character, while muted tones might better represent a more somber figure.

2. Functionality

Puppet costumes must also be functional. The materials used should allow for ease of movement, ensuring that the puppet can perform its actions without hindrance. Consider how the costume will interact with the puppet's mechanics. For example, if the puppet has moving arms, the sleeves should be designed to accommodate this movement without becoming restrictive.

3. Visual Impact

Costumes should be visually striking, capturing the audience's attention from the moment the puppet enters the stage. Think about how the costume will look from a distance, as well as up close. Bold patterns, contrasting colors, and unique textures can create a memorable visual impression that enhances the character's appeal.

4. Cultural Context

Understanding the cultural context of your character can greatly influence costume design. If your puppet is inspired by a specific culture or historical period, research traditional garments and styles to ensure authenticity. This not only enriches the character but also shows respect for the culture being represented.

5. Layering and Texture

Layering can add depth and interest to a puppet's costume. Consider using multiple layers of fabric to create a sense of dimension. Different textures can also enhance the visual experience; for example, combining smooth satin with rough burlap can create a striking contrast that draws the eye.

Fabric Choices

The selection of fabrics is a crucial aspect of costume design, as it directly impacts the puppet's appearance, movement, and overall character portrayal. Each fabric carries its own unique qualities, and understanding these can elevate your puppet's costume from ordinary to extraordinary.

1. Types of Fabrics

When choosing fabrics, consider the following options:

- Cotton: A versatile and breathable fabric, cotton is ideal for a wide range of puppet costumes. It can be easily dyed and printed, allowing for vibrant designs. Cotton is also durable, making it suitable for puppets that will be handled frequently.

- Felt: This fabric is excellent for creating whimsical characters. Felt is easy to work with, does not fray, and can be cut into intricate shapes. Its stiffness allows for structural elements, such as hats or wings, to hold their shape.

- Silk: For a touch of elegance, silk can be used to create luxurious costumes. Its natural sheen adds a sophisticated element, perfect for characters that embody grace and refinement. However, silk requires careful handling and may not be the best choice for puppets that will undergo rigorous movement.

- Tulle: This lightweight, sheer fabric is perfect for creating ethereal costumes. Tulle can be layered to add volume and texture, making it ideal for fairy or fantasy characters. Its delicate nature allows for a whimsical appearance that can enchant audiences.

- Velvet: Known for its rich texture and depth of color, velvet can add a dramatic flair to puppet costumes. It is particularly effective for characters that exude luxury or mystery. However, velvet can be heavier, so consider the puppet's mechanics when using this fabric.

2. Color Theory

Color plays a vital role in costume design, influencing the audience's perception of the character. Understanding color theory can help you make informed choices that enhance the character's personality and emotional resonance.

- Warm Colors: Reds, oranges, and yellows evoke feelings of warmth, energy, and excitement. These colors are perfect for lively characters that embody joy and enthusiasm.

- Cool Colors: Blues, greens, and purples convey calmness, tranquility, and introspection. These hues are suitable for characters that are more subdued or contemplative.

- Neutral Colors: Whites, blacks, and grays can serve as a backdrop for more vibrant colors or can be used to represent characters that are grounded or serious.

Consider how the colors you choose will interact with one another. Complementary colors can create visual harmony, while contrasting colors can add drama and tension.

3. Patterns and Prints

Patterns and prints can add an extra layer of character to your puppet's costume. Stripes, polka dots, florals, and geometric designs can all contribute to the character's identity. When selecting patterns, consider the following:

- Scale: The scale of the pattern can impact how it reads from a distance. Larger patterns may be more visible from afar, while smaller patterns can add detail that is appreciated up close.

- Theme: Ensure that the patterns align with the character's theme. For example, a puppet representing nature may benefit from floral prints, while a futuristic character might suit geometric designs.

- Mixing Patterns: Mixing patterns can create a dynamic look, but it requires careful consideration. Aim for a cohesive color palette to ensure that the patterns complement rather than clash with one another.

Accessorizing Characters

Accessories are the finishing touches that can elevate a puppet's costume from good to unforgettable. They provide opportunities for creativity and can help to further define the character's personality and story.

1. Types of Accessories

Consider incorporating the following types of accessories into your puppet's costume:

- Hats: A well-chosen hat can instantly convey a character's personality. Whether it's a whimsical top hat, a practical cap, or a regal crown, hats can add a distinctive flair.

- Jewelry: Necklaces, bracelets, and earrings can enhance a puppet's costume, adding sparkle and interest. Choose pieces that align with the character's style; for instance, a pirate puppet might wear a simple leather necklace, while a princess puppet could don a sparkling tiara.

- Props: Props can serve as extensions of the character, providing context and enhancing storytelling. A puppet holding a musical instrument, a book, or a magical wand can communicate its role in the narrative.

- Footwear: While puppets may not always require shoes, adding footwear can contribute to the overall look. Consider the character's environment and personality when selecting shoes; a rugged character might wear boots, while a fairy might have delicate slippers.

2. Personalization

Personalizing accessories can make your puppet feel more unique and relatable. Consider adding elements that reflect the character's backstory or interests. For example, a puppet that loves gardening might wear a flower crown or carry a small watering can.

3. Balance and Proportion

When accessorizing, it's essential to maintain balance and proportion. Accessories should enhance the character without overwhelming it. A large hat may require smaller accessories to create harmony, while a simple costume may benefit from bolder accessories to draw attention.

4. Practical Considerations

Finally, consider the practicality of the accessories. Ensure that they do not impede the puppet's movement or functionality. Accessories should be securely attached and lightweight, allowing for seamless performance.

Chapter 19: Building a Puppet from Scratch

Creating a puppet from scratch is a delightful journey that allows you to express your creativity while honing your craftsmanship. This chapter will guide you through the essential materials, a step-by-step process, and valuable tips to help you embark on this artistic endeavor. Whether you are a novice or have some experience, the joy of bringing a character to life with your own hands is an experience like no other.

Materials Needed

To begin your puppet-making adventure, gather the following materials. Each item plays a crucial role in the construction and character of your puppet, so choose wisely and with intention.

1. Base Structure

The base structure of your puppet can be made from various materials, depending on the type of puppet you wish to create. Common options include:

- Wood: Lightweight and sturdy, wood is ideal for marionettes and rod puppets. Balsa wood is particularly easy to work with for beginners.

- Foam: Soft and versatile, foam can be shaped and carved to create a lightweight puppet body. It is especially popular for hand puppets.

- Cardboard: An accessible and inexpensive option, cardboard can be used for simple puppets, especially for children's projects.

- Plastic: For more durable puppets, consider using plastic materials, which can withstand wear and tear.

2. Fabric and Textiles

Selecting the right fabric is essential for the puppet's appearance and texture. Consider the following:

- Felt: Easy to cut and sew, felt is perfect for creating vibrant and colorful puppets.

- Cotton: Soft and breathable, cotton fabric can be used for clothing and puppet skin.

- Satin or Silk: For a more luxurious look, satin or silk can add elegance to your puppet's costume.

3. Adhesives and Fasteners

To assemble your puppet, you will need reliable adhesives and fasteners. Options include:

- Hot Glue Gun: A staple in puppet-making, a hot glue gun provides a strong bond for various materials.

- Fabric Glue: Ideal for attaching fabric pieces, fabric glue dries clear and is flexible.

- Sewing Supplies: Needles, thread, and scissors are essential for sewing fabric parts together.

4. Features and Accessories

To give your puppet personality, consider adding features and accessories:

- Eyes: Use googly eyes, buttons, or fabric to create expressive eyes.

- Hair: Yarn, feathers, or faux fur can be used to create hair or other headpieces.

- Costumes: Design and sew costumes that reflect your puppet's character.

5. Tools

Having the right tools will make your puppet-building process smoother:

- Scissors: A good pair of scissors is essential for cutting fabric and other materials.

- Craft Knife: For precision cutting, especially with cardboard or foam.

- Ruler and Measuring Tape: Accurate measurements are crucial for a well-proportioned puppet.

Step-by-Step Guide

Now that you have gathered your materials, let's delve into the step-by-step process of building your puppet from scratch. Follow these instructions carefully, and don't hesitate to infuse your unique style into each step.

Step 1: Conceptualize Your Puppet

Before you start building, take a moment to conceptualize your puppet. What character do you want to create? Consider their personality, backstory, and appearance. Sketch your ideas on paper, focusing on the puppet's shape, size, and features. This initial design will serve as your blueprint.

Step 2: Create the Base Structure

Using your chosen base material, begin constructing the puppet's body. If you are making a hand puppet, cut out a simple shape that will fit comfortably over your hand. For a marionette, create a torso and limbs separately, ensuring they can be attached later.

- For a Hand Puppet: Cut a piece of fabric that is large enough to cover your hand and extend to form the puppet's head and body. Sew or glue the edges to create a pocket for your hand.

- For a Marionette: Cut out the torso from wood or foam, and create limbs that can be attached with string or rods. Ensure the joints allow for movement.

Step 3: Add Features

Once the base structure is complete, it's time to add features that bring your puppet to life. Start with the face:

- Eyes: Attach your chosen eyes securely. If using buttons or googly eyes, glue them in place. For fabric eyes, sew or glue them on.

- Mouth: Create a mouth by cutting a slit in the fabric or using a separate piece that can open and close. This will allow for expression and speech.

- Hair: Attach hair using yarn or other materials. Experiment with different styles to match your puppet's personality.

Step 4: Dress Your Puppet

Design and create a costume that reflects your puppet's character. Use fabric scraps to sew or glue clothing onto your puppet. Consider layering different fabrics for added texture and visual interest. Accessories like hats, scarves, or jewelry can enhance your puppet's personality.

Step 5: Assemble the Puppet

If you are creating a marionette, now is the time to assemble the limbs. Attach strings or rods to the joints, ensuring they are balanced for smooth movement. For hand puppets, ensure all parts are securely attached and that the puppet fits comfortably on your hand.

Step 6: Test Movement and Expression

Once your puppet is assembled, it's essential to test its movement and expression. Practice manipulating the puppet to see how it moves and responds. Adjust the strings or joints as necessary to achieve the desired range of motion.

Step 7: Final Touches

Add any final touches to your puppet. This could include additional details like makeup, extra accessories, or even a name tag. Personalizing your puppet will make it feel more complete and ready for performance.

Tips for Beginners

As you embark on your puppet-making journey, consider these tips to enhance your experience and results.

1. Start Simple

If you are new to puppet-making, begin with a simple design. A basic hand puppet or sock puppet can be a great starting point. As you gain confidence, you can explore more complex designs.

2. Experiment with Materials

Don't be afraid to experiment with different materials. Each material offers unique textures and possibilities. Try combining fabrics, using unconventional items, or even recycling materials to create something truly original.

3. Embrace Mistakes

Mistakes are a natural part of the creative process. If something doesn't turn out as planned, view it as an opportunity to learn and improve. Adapt your design or technique, and remember that every artist has faced challenges.

4. Seek Inspiration

Look for inspiration in various places. Attend puppet shows, watch films featuring puppetry, or browse online galleries. Observing other puppeteers can spark ideas and help you refine your own style.

5. Join a Community

Engaging with other puppet enthusiasts can be incredibly rewarding. Join local puppet-making groups, attend workshops, or participate in online forums. Sharing experiences and techniques with others can enhance your skills and provide valuable feedback.

6. Practice Regularly

Like any art form, practice is key to improvement. Set aside time to work on your puppetry skills regularly. The more you create, the more confident and skilled you will become.

7. Have Fun!

Above all, remember to have fun! Puppet-making is an opportunity to express yourself and explore your creativity. Enjoy the process, and let your imagination run wild as you bring your characters to life.

Chapter 20: Using Technology in Puppetry

Digital Puppetry

Digital puppetry represents a fascinating intersection of traditional puppetry and modern technology, allowing artists to explore new dimensions of character creation and performance. This innovative approach harnesses the power of digital tools to breathe life into puppets in ways that were previously unimaginable. At its core, digital puppetry utilizes software and hardware to manipulate virtual puppets in real-time. This can range from simple animations to complex performances that integrate live actors and digital avatars. The advent of motion capture technology has revolutionized this field, enabling puppeteers to translate their movements into the digital realm seamlessly. One of the most significant advantages of digital puppetry is the ability to create characters that defy the laws of physics. A puppet can fly, morph, or even change its appearance instantaneously, captivating audiences with visual spectacles that traditional puppetry might struggle to achieve. This freedom allows for a broader range of storytelling possibilities, where the only limit is the imagination of the creator. Moreover, digital puppetry can enhance the emotional depth of characters. By employing sophisticated animation techniques, artists can imbue their puppets with nuanced expressions and movements that resonate with audiences on a deeper level. The subtleties of a raised eyebrow or a slight tilt of the head can convey a wealth of information about a character's feelings and intentions, enriching the narrative experience. As we delve into the world of digital puppetry, it is essential to consider the tools and software that have become staples in this evolving art form. Programs such as Adobe Character Animator, Unity, and Blender have opened new avenues for creators to design, animate, and perform with their digital puppets. These platforms offer a range of features that allow for real-time manipulation, making it easier than ever to bring characters to life. In addition to software, hardware plays a crucial role in digital puppetry. Devices such as motion capture suits, webcams, and specialized controllers enable puppeteers to interact with their digital creations in intuitive ways. The integration of augmented reality (AR) and virtual reality (VR) technologies further enhances this experience, allowing audiences to engage with puppetry in immersive environments. As we explore the realm of digital puppetry, it is vital to recognize the importance of storytelling. While technology provides new tools for expression, the heart of puppetry remains the narrative. Successful digital puppetry combines technical skill with compelling storytelling, ensuring that characters resonate with audiences and evoke genuine emotions.

Animation Techniques

Animation techniques in puppetry have evolved dramatically, offering artists a plethora of methods to create dynamic and engaging characters. Understanding these techniques is essential for any puppeteer looking to enhance their craft and push the boundaries of their creations. One of the foundational techniques in animation is keyframing. This method involves setting specific points in time where a puppet's position, rotation, or scale changes. By defining these keyframes, animators can create smooth transitions and lifelike movements. The beauty of keyframing lies in its versatility; it can be applied to both traditional and digital puppetry, allowing for a seamless blend of techniques. Another popular technique is rigging, which involves creating a skeletal structure for a puppet. This structure allows for more complex movements and poses, as the animator can manipulate the rig to achieve desired actions. Rigging is particularly beneficial in digital puppetry, where the intricacies of a character's movement can be controlled with precision. In addition to keyframing and rigging, animators often employ the technique of tweening. This process involves generating intermediate frames between two keyframes, resulting in smooth transitions and fluid motion. Tweening can save time and effort, allowing artists to focus on the creative aspects of their work while ensuring that movements appear natural and cohesive. The use of stop-motion animation is another captivating technique in puppetry. This method involves photographing a puppet in various positions and then compiling these images to create the illusion of movement. Stop-motion animation has a unique charm, as it captures the tactile quality of physical puppets, inviting audiences into a world where characters are crafted with care and attention to detail. In the realm of digital puppetry, 3D animation techniques have gained prominence. Artists can create intricate models and animate them using software like Maya or Cinema 4D. This approach allows for a high degree of realism and detail, enabling characters to exhibit a wide range of emotions and expressions. To illustrate the various animation techniques, the following table summarizes key methods and their applications:

Technique	Description	Applications
Keyframing	Setting specific points in time for puppet movement.	Traditional and digital puppetry.
Rigging	Creating a skeletal structure for complex movements.	Digital puppetry, 3D animation.
Tweening	Generating intermediate frames for smooth transitions.	Animation in both digital and traditional puppetry.
Stop-Motion Animation	Photographing puppets in various positions to create movement.	Traditional puppetry, film, and television.
3D Animation	Creating and animating intricate 3D models.	Digital puppetry, video games, and films.

Each of these techniques offers unique opportunities for character creation and storytelling. By mastering these methods, puppeteers can elevate their performances and engage audiences in new and exciting ways.

Interactive Elements

Incorporating interactive elements into puppetry has transformed the way audiences engage with characters and stories. This innovative approach invites viewers to participate actively in the performance, creating a dynamic and immersive experience that transcends traditional boundaries. One of the most effective ways to introduce interactivity is through audience participation. This can take many forms, from inviting children on stage to interact with puppets to incorporating live polls or decision-making moments that influence the direction of the story. By allowing the audience to become part of the narrative, puppeteers can foster a sense of connection and investment in the characters and their journeys. Technology plays a pivotal role in enhancing interactivity in puppetry. For instance, the use of mobile applications can allow audience members to interact with puppets through their devices. These apps can provide additional content, such as character backstories, games, or augmented reality experiences that bring puppets to life in new and exciting ways. This integration of technology not only enriches the performance but also extends the experience beyond the theater, allowing audiences to engage with characters long after the show has ended. Another fascinating aspect of interactive puppetry is the use of sensors and responsive technology. By equipping puppets with sensors, puppeteers can create characters that react to audience input, such as sound or movement. This responsiveness adds an element of surprise and spontaneity to performances, as characters can adapt to the energy and reactions of the audience in real-time. The following table highlights various interactive elements that can be incorporated into puppetry performances:

Interactive Element	Description	Benefits
Audience Participation	Inviting audience members to engage directly with puppets.	Fosters connection and investment in the story.
Mobile Applications	Using apps to provide additional content and experiences.	Extends engagement beyond the performance.
Sensors and Responsive Technology	Equipping puppets with sensors to react to audience input.	Adds spontaneity and surprise to performances.
Interactive Storytelling	Allowing audiences to influence the direction of the narrative.	Creates a unique experience for each performance.
Virtual Reality Experiences	Immersive environments where audiences can interact with puppets.	Enhances engagement and creates memorable experiences.

As we embrace the potential of interactive elements in puppetry, it is essential to maintain a balance between technology and storytelling. While interactivity can enhance the experience, the core of puppetry lies in the narrative and the characters that inhabit it. By thoughtfully integrating interactive elements, puppeteers can create performances that resonate with audiences and leave a lasting impact.

Chapter 21: The Ethics of Puppetry

Respecting Cultures

In the vibrant tapestry of puppetry, the threads of culture weave intricate patterns that reflect the diversity of human experience. Puppetry has long served as a medium through which stories are told, traditions are preserved, and communities are engaged. However, with this power comes a profound responsibility to respect the cultures from which these stories originate. When creating puppet characters that draw inspiration from specific cultural backgrounds, it is essential to approach the task with sensitivity and awareness. This begins with thorough research. Understanding the historical, social, and artistic contexts of a culture can illuminate the nuances that make it unique. Engaging with cultural representatives, artists, and scholars can provide invaluable insights that enrich the character creation process. For instance, consider the rich tradition of shadow puppetry in Indonesia, known as Wayang Kulit. This art form is not merely a performance; it is a reflection of the values, beliefs, and narratives of the Javanese people. A puppeteer seeking to create a character inspired by this tradition must delve into its origins, the significance of its stories, and the symbolism embedded in its puppets. By doing so, the puppeteer honors the culture and contributes to its ongoing narrative rather than appropriating it. Moreover, respecting cultures involves recognizing the power dynamics at play. Historically, many cultures have been marginalized or misrepresented in mainstream media. Puppetry, as an accessible and engaging art form, can either perpetuate stereotypes or serve as a platform for authentic representation. It is crucial to ensure that the voices of those from the culture being represented are included in the creative process. This collaboration not only enriches the character but also fosters a sense of community and respect. In addition, the visual representation of characters must be approached with care. The design of a puppet should reflect the cultural aesthetics accurately and respectfully. This includes considerations of color, materials, and traditional motifs. A puppet that embodies the spirit of a culture can serve as a bridge, inviting audiences to explore and appreciate its richness. Ultimately, respecting cultures in puppetry is about creating a dialogue rather than a monologue. It is about listening, learning, and sharing. By embracing this ethos, puppeteers can create characters that resonate with authenticity and foster a deeper understanding of the diverse world we inhabit.

Avoiding Stereotypes

Stereotypes can be insidious, creeping into narratives and character designs in ways that are often unintentional yet profoundly damaging. In the realm of puppetry, where visual representation plays a pivotal role, it is imperative to be vigilant against the perpetuation of stereotypes. Stereotypes reduce complex individuals and cultures to simplistic caricatures, stripping away the richness of their stories and experiences. When crafting puppet characters, it is essential to move beyond clichés and explore the multifaceted nature of identity. This involves recognizing that every character, regardless of their cultural background, is a unique amalgamation of traits, experiences, and emotions. One effective strategy for avoiding stereotypes is to engage in character development that prioritizes depth over superficiality. Instead of relying on broad generalizations, puppeteers can create characters with distinct personalities, motivations, and arcs. For example, rather than depicting a character from a specific culture solely as a "wise elder" or "comic relief," consider their individual journey, struggles, and triumphs. This approach not only enriches the character but also invites audiences to connect with them on a more profound level. Furthermore, it is crucial to challenge one's own biases and assumptions during the character creation process. This requires introspection and a willingness to confront uncomfortable truths about how certain cultures are often portrayed. Engaging with diverse perspectives can illuminate blind spots and foster a more nuanced understanding of the characters being created. In addition, collaboration with artists and storytellers from the cultures being represented can provide essential guidance in avoiding stereotypes. Their insights can help ensure that the characters are portrayed authentically and respectfully. This collaborative approach not only enhances the quality of the puppetry but also builds bridges between communities. Ultimately, avoiding stereotypes in puppetry is about embracing complexity and celebrating diversity. It is about recognizing that every character has a story worth telling and that these stories deserve to be shared with authenticity and respect.

Responsible Storytelling

At the heart of puppetry lies the art of storytelling, a powerful tool that can shape perceptions, challenge norms, and inspire change. As puppeteers embark on the journey of character creation, the ethical implications of their narratives must be at the forefront of their minds. Responsible storytelling is not merely a guideline; it is a commitment to integrity, empathy, and social consciousness. Responsible storytelling begins with an understanding of the impact that narratives can have on audiences. Stories can reinforce existing stereotypes, perpetuate harmful myths, or, conversely, they can illuminate truths and foster understanding. Puppeteers have the unique opportunity to craft narratives that resonate with audiences while also promoting empathy and inclusivity. One key aspect of responsible storytelling is the representation of diverse voices. It is essential to amplify the stories of those who have historically been marginalized or silenced. This can be achieved by creating puppet characters that reflect a wide range of experiences, backgrounds, and perspectives. By doing so, puppeteers can challenge the dominant narratives that often overshadow the richness of human experience. Moreover, the themes explored in puppet shows should be approached with care and thoughtfulness. Sensitive topics such as race, gender, and social justice require a nuanced understanding and a commitment to authenticity. Puppeteers should strive to create narratives that not only entertain but also provoke thought and inspire dialogue. This may involve tackling difficult subjects with sensitivity, ensuring that the portrayal of characters and their experiences is both respectful and enlightening. In addition, the context in which a puppet show is presented plays a significant role in responsible storytelling. Consideration should be given to the audience's background, cultural context, and potential sensitivities. This awareness can guide the puppeteer in crafting narratives that resonate positively and avoid unintentional harm. Furthermore, feedback from audiences and community members can be invaluable in refining narratives and ensuring that they are responsible and respectful. Engaging in open dialogue with viewers can provide insights into how stories are perceived and the impact they have. This iterative process of feedback and reflection can lead to more thoughtful and impactful storytelling. Ultimately, responsible storytelling in puppetry is about recognizing the power of narratives to shape perceptions and foster understanding. It is a commitment to creating characters and stories that reflect the complexity of the human experience while promoting empathy, inclusivity, and social consciousness. By embracing this responsibility, puppeteers can contribute to a richer, more diverse tapestry of storytelling that resonates with audiences of all backgrounds.

Chapter 22: Creating a Puppet Show Script

Creating a puppet show script is an intricate dance of creativity, structure, and emotional resonance. It is the blueprint that guides the performance, allowing the puppeteer to breathe life into their characters and convey a story that resonates with the audience. In this chapter, we will explore the essential components of scriptwriting for puppetry, focusing on the structure of a script, the art of dialogue writing, and the development of engaging scenes.

Structure of a Script

The structure of a puppet show script serves as the backbone of the performance. A well-structured script not only organizes the narrative but also enhances the pacing and flow of the show. Typically, a puppet show script can be divided into three main acts, mirroring the classic three-act structure found in many forms of storytelling.

The following table outlines the key components of each act:

Act	Purpose	Key Elements
Act 1	Introduction	Establish characters, setting, and conflict
Act 2	Development	Deepen conflict, develop relationships, introduce obstacles
Act 3	Resolution	Resolve conflict, conclude character arcs, provide closure

Each act should be carefully crafted to ensure that the audience remains engaged. The first act sets the stage, introducing the characters and the world they inhabit. It is crucial to hook the audience's attention early on, as this will determine their investment in the story.

In the second act, the plot thickens. This is where the characters face challenges and conflicts that test their resolve. It is essential to create tension and suspense, keeping the audience on the edge of their seats. The relationships between characters should evolve, revealing deeper layers of their personalities and motivations.

Finally, the third act brings resolution. Here, the conflicts are addressed, and the characters undergo transformation. The audience should leave feeling satisfied, having witnessed a journey that resonates with them on a personal level.

Dialogue Writing

Dialogue is the lifeblood of any script, especially in puppetry, where the characters must convey emotion and personality through their words. Writing effective dialogue requires an understanding of each character's voice, background, and motivations.

When crafting dialogue for puppets, consider the following elements:

Character Voice

Each puppet should have a distinct voice that reflects its personality. A wise old owl may speak in a slow, deliberate manner, while a mischievous monkey might use quick, playful language. To achieve this, consider the following:

- Vocabulary: Choose words that align with the character's background and personality. A sophisticated character may use more complex language, while a childlike character may use simpler words.

- Tone: The tone of the dialogue should match the character's emotional state. A character in distress may speak in short, fragmented sentences, while a confident character may use longer, more fluid sentences.

Subtext

Effective dialogue often contains subtext—what is unsaid but implied. This adds depth to the characters and their interactions. For example, a character may say, "I'm fine," while their body language and tone suggest otherwise. This creates a richer experience for the audience, who can read between the lines.

Rhythm and Pacing

The rhythm of dialogue can greatly impact the flow of the performance. Varying the length of sentences and the speed of delivery can create tension or humor. Quick exchanges can heighten excitement, while slower dialogue can allow for reflection and emotional depth.

Scene Development

Scenes are the building blocks of a puppet show, each contributing to the overall narrative arc. Developing scenes requires careful consideration of setting, action, and character interaction.

Setting the Scene

The setting provides context for the action and influences the mood of the scene. When writing a scene, consider the following:

- Location: Where does the scene take place? A bustling marketplace will have a different energy than a quiet forest glade.

- Time: What time of day is it? The lighting and atmosphere can significantly impact the scene's tone.

- Visual Elements: Describe the visual elements that will be represented by the puppets and the stage. This includes props, backdrops, and any other elements that enhance the storytelling.

Action and Movement

Puppetry is a visual medium, and the action within a scene should be dynamic and engaging. Consider how the puppets will move and interact with each other and their environment. This can include:

- Choreography: Plan the movements of the puppets to ensure they are fluid and natural. This may involve rehearsing specific actions to achieve the desired effect.

- Interaction: How do the characters interact with one another? Dialogue should be complemented by physical actions that enhance the emotional impact of the scene.

Character Interaction

The interactions between characters are crucial to driving the narrative forward. Each scene should reveal something new about the characters or advance the plot. Consider the following:

- Conflict: What conflicts arise between characters? This can create tension and keep the audience engaged.

- Resolution: How do characters resolve their differences? This can lead to character growth and development.

In summary, creating a puppet show script is a multifaceted process that requires careful attention to structure, dialogue, and scene development. By understanding the intricacies of scriptwriting, puppeteers can craft compelling narratives that resonate with audiences of all ages. The art of puppetry is not just about the puppets themselves; it is about the stories they tell and the connections they forge with those who watch.

As you embark on your journey to create a puppet show script, remember to infuse your unique voice and vision into every word. The world of puppetry is a canvas waiting for your creativity to bring it to life.

Chapter 23: The Role of Lighting in Puppetry

Lighting is an essential element in the art of puppetry, serving not only to illuminate the stage but also to enhance the emotional resonance of the performance. It is a powerful tool that can transform a simple puppet show into a captivating experience, drawing the audience into the world of the characters. In this chapter, we will explore the multifaceted role of lighting in puppetry, examining how it can set the mood, highlight characters, and employ practical techniques to elevate the overall performance.

Setting the Mood

The atmosphere of a puppet show is intricately woven through the use of lighting. It is the first brushstroke on the canvas of a performance, establishing the tone and inviting the audience into a specific emotional landscape. Whether it is the warm glow of a sunset or the eerie shadows of a moonlit night, lighting can evoke feelings that resonate deeply within the viewer. Consider the opening scene of a whimsical tale. Soft, diffused lighting can create a sense of wonder and enchantment, drawing the audience into a world of imagination. The gentle play of light can mimic the soft caress of a breeze, inviting viewers to suspend their disbelief and embrace the magic of the moment. In contrast, a stark, harsh light can evoke tension and unease, setting the stage for a dramatic confrontation or a moment of revelation. The color of the light also plays a crucial role in mood setting. Warm hues, such as soft yellows and oranges, can evoke feelings of comfort and joy, while cooler tones, like blues and greens, can instill a sense of calm or melancholy. By manipulating color temperature, puppeteers can guide the audience's emotional journey, subtly influencing their reactions to the unfolding narrative. Moreover, the intensity of the light can create dynamic shifts in mood. A gradual dimming can signal a transition from a lively scene to a more introspective moment, allowing the audience to reflect on the characters' emotions. Conversely, a sudden spotlight can heighten the drama of a pivotal scene, capturing the audience's attention and drawing them into the heart of the action. Lighting can also be used to create contrasts that enhance storytelling. For instance, a brightly lit foreground can juxtapose a shadowy background, symbolizing the struggle between light and darkness, hope and despair. This interplay of light and shadow can add layers of meaning to the performance, inviting the audience to engage with the narrative on a deeper level. In essence, lighting is not merely a technical aspect of puppetry; it is an artistic expression that shapes the audience's experience. By thoughtfully crafting the lighting design, puppeteers can create an immersive environment that resonates with the emotions of the characters and the themes of the story.

Highlighting Characters

In puppetry, characters are the heart of the performance, and lighting serves as a vital tool for bringing them to life. By strategically illuminating the puppets, puppeteers can draw the audience's focus to specific characters, enhancing their presence and emotional impact. A well-placed spotlight can transform a puppet into a larger-than-life figure, commanding the audience's attention. This technique is particularly effective during moments of revelation or emotional intensity, where the character's expression and movements are paramount. By isolating a character in light, the puppeteer can emphasize their significance within the narrative, allowing the audience to connect more deeply with their journey. Furthermore, lighting can be used to convey character traits and emotions. For instance, a character who embodies joy and exuberance may be bathed in bright, vibrant light, while a more introspective or troubled character might be shrouded in softer, muted tones. This visual representation of character traits not only enhances the storytelling but also allows the audience to intuitively grasp the essence of each puppet. The interplay of light and shadow can also be employed to create depth and dimension in character portrayal. By casting shadows that mimic the puppet's movements, puppeteers can add a layer of complexity to the performance. This technique can be particularly effective in conveying internal conflict or emotional turmoil, as the shadows may reflect the character's struggles, enhancing the audience's understanding of their journey. Moreover, lighting can facilitate character interactions, highlighting relationships and dynamics between puppets. For example, a warm, shared light can symbolize camaraderie and connection, while contrasting lighting can underscore tension or conflict. By illuminating characters in relation to one another, puppeteers can visually represent the nuances of their relationships, enriching the narrative and engaging the audience on multiple levels. In addition to enhancing character portrayal, lighting can also serve to establish the physical space in which the characters exist. By creating distinct lighting zones, puppeteers can delineate different areas of the stage, guiding the audience's attention and shaping their understanding of the story's geography. This spatial awareness is crucial in puppetry, where the audience's perception of the characters' environment can significantly impact their engagement with the narrative.

Ultimately, the thoughtful use of lighting to highlight characters is an essential aspect of puppetry that elevates the performance from mere entertainment to a profound artistic experience. By illuminating the puppets in ways that resonate with their personalities and relationships, puppeteers can create a rich tapestry of storytelling that captivates the audience's imagination.

Practical Techniques

While the artistic aspects of lighting in puppetry are essential, practical techniques also play a crucial role in achieving effective lighting design. Understanding the tools and methods available to puppeteers can enhance their ability to create captivating visual experiences. One of the fundamental techniques in puppetry lighting is the use of different types of lights. Spotlights, floodlights, and LED fixtures each offer unique qualities that can be harnessed to achieve specific effects. Spotlights are ideal for highlighting individual characters or moments, while floodlights provide a broader wash of light that can illuminate the entire stage. LED fixtures, with their versatility and color-changing capabilities, allow for dynamic lighting effects that can shift throughout the performance. In addition to the type of lighting used, the placement of lights is crucial in shaping the overall visual experience. Front lighting can create a flat, even illumination that is effective for general visibility, while side lighting adds depth and dimension, enhancing the three-dimensionality of the puppets. Backlighting can create striking silhouettes, adding drama and intrigue to the performance. By experimenting with different lighting angles, puppeteers can discover the most effective ways to showcase their characters and the story. Color gels are another practical tool that can transform the lighting design. By placing colored filters over lights, puppeteers can create a wide range of moods and atmospheres. For instance, a red gel can evoke feelings of passion or danger, while a blue gel can instill a sense of calm or sadness. The careful selection of color gels can enhance the emotional impact of the performance, allowing the audience to connect more deeply with the characters and their journeys. Incorporating dimmers and control systems can further enhance the puppeteer's ability to manipulate lighting in real-time. Dimmers allow for gradual changes in intensity, enabling smooth transitions between scenes and moods. Control systems can facilitate complex lighting cues, allowing for precise timing and coordination with the performance. This level of control empowers puppeteers to create a seamless integration of lighting with the narrative, enhancing the overall impact of the show. Additionally, puppeteers can explore the use of projections and visual effects to complement their lighting design. By incorporating projected images or animations, they can create immersive environments that transport the audience into different worlds. This technique can be particularly effective in enhancing storytelling, as it adds layers of visual interest that engage the audience's imagination.

Collaboration with lighting designers can also elevate the puppetry experience. Working together, puppeteers and lighting designers can brainstorm innovative ideas and explore creative possibilities that enhance the performance. This collaborative approach can lead to unique lighting solutions that align with the artistic vision of the puppeteer, resulting in a cohesive and captivating show.

Chapter 24: Marketing Your Puppet Characters

Marketing puppet characters is an art form in itself, requiring a blend of creativity, strategy, and an understanding of the audience. In this chapter, we will explore the essential components of effectively promoting your puppet creations, ensuring they resonate with viewers and stand out in a crowded marketplace.

Branding

Branding is the cornerstone of any successful marketing strategy. It encompasses the visual identity, voice, and personality of your puppet characters, creating a memorable impression that lingers in the minds of your audience.

Defining Your Brand Identity

To establish a strong brand identity, begin by defining the core values and mission of your puppet characters. What do they represent? What emotions do you want to evoke in your audience? Consider the following elements:

Element	Questions to Consider
Character Traits	What are the defining traits of your puppet? Are they humorous, wise, mischievous?
Visual Style	What colors, shapes, and designs best represent your character? How do they stand out?
Voice and Tone	What kind of voice does your puppet have? Is it playful, serious, or whimsical?
Target Audience	Who are you trying to reach? Children, adults, or a specific community?

By answering these questions, you can create a cohesive brand identity that resonates with your audience.

Creating a Visual Identity

The visual identity of your puppet characters is crucial for effective branding. This includes the design of the puppets themselves, as well as any promotional materials you create. Consider the following aspects:

- Logo Design: A unique logo can encapsulate the essence of your puppet characters. It should be simple yet memorable, easily recognizable across various platforms.

- Color Palette: Choose a color palette that reflects the personality of your characters. Bright, vibrant colors may appeal to children, while more muted tones might resonate with adult audiences.

- Typography: The font you choose for any written materials should align with your brand's voice. Playful fonts can convey a sense of fun, while elegant fonts may suggest sophistication.

Consistency Across Platforms

Once you have established your brand identity, it is essential to maintain consistency across all platforms. This includes your website, social media profiles, and any promotional materials. Consistent branding helps build trust and recognition among your audience.

Social Media Strategies

In today's digital age, social media is an invaluable tool for marketing puppet characters. It allows for direct engagement with your audience and provides a platform to showcase your creations.

Choosing the Right Platforms

Not all social media platforms are created equal. Each platform has its unique audience and style. Consider the following when choosing where to promote your puppet characters:

Platform	Best For
Instagram	Visual storytelling through images and videos. Ideal for showcasing puppet designs and performances.
Facebook	Building community and sharing longer content. Great for event promotion and audience engagement.
Twitter	Quick updates and engaging in conversations. Useful for connecting with other artists and audiences.
YouTube	Video content showcasing performances, tutorials, and behind-the-scenes looks. Perfect for reaching a wider audience.

Content Creation

Creating engaging content is key to attracting and retaining an audience. Here are some ideas for content that can help promote your puppet characters:

- Behind-the-Scenes Videos: Share the process of creating your puppets, from design to performance. This transparency can foster a deeper connection with your audience.

- Character Introductions: Create short videos introducing your puppet characters, highlighting their unique traits and backstories.

- Interactive Content: Engage your audience with polls, quizzes, or challenges related to your puppet characters. This can encourage participation and build community.

Engagement and Community Building

Social media is not just about broadcasting your content; it's also about engaging with your audience. Respond to comments, ask for feedback, and encourage discussions about your puppet characters. Building a community around your brand can lead to loyal followers who are invested in your work.

Building an Audience

Building an audience for your puppet characters is a gradual process that requires dedication and creativity. Here are some strategies to help you grow your following.

Networking with Other Artists

Connecting with other puppeteers and artists can open doors to new opportunities. Attend workshops, festivals, and conventions to meet like-minded individuals. Collaborations can lead to cross-promotion, expanding your audience reach.

Participating in Events

Participating in local events, festivals, or community gatherings can provide exposure for your puppet characters. Performances, workshops, or interactive sessions can attract attention and create memorable experiences for attendees.

Utilizing Email Marketing

Building an email list allows you to communicate directly with your audience. Share updates, upcoming performances, and exclusive content with your subscribers. Email marketing can be a powerful tool for nurturing relationships and keeping your audience engaged.

Offering Merchandise

Consider creating merchandise related to your puppet characters, such as plush toys, apparel, or art prints. This not only serves as an additional revenue stream but also helps promote your brand. Fans are more likely to share their purchases on social media, further expanding your reach.

Tracking and Analyzing Your Efforts

Finally, it's essential to track the effectiveness of your marketing strategies. Use analytics tools to monitor engagement, audience growth, and the success of your campaigns. This data can inform future marketing decisions and help you refine your approach.

Chapter 25: The Impact of Puppetry on Education

Educational Benefits

Puppetry, an age-old art form, has found its way into the modern educational landscape, proving to be a powerful tool for teaching and learning. The benefits of incorporating puppetry into educational settings are manifold, extending beyond mere entertainment to foster a rich environment for cognitive, emotional, and social development. At its core, puppetry engages students in a unique manner, allowing them to explore complex concepts through a medium that is both accessible and enjoyable. The act of creating and manipulating puppets encourages creativity, critical thinking, and problem-solving skills. Students are not just passive recipients of information; they become active participants in their learning journey. This hands-on approach fosters a deeper understanding of the material, as students are more likely to remember and internalize lessons when they are involved in the process. Moreover, puppetry serves as an excellent medium for storytelling, a fundamental aspect of education. Through the use of puppets, educators can bring stories to life, making abstract ideas tangible and relatable. This narrative approach helps students to connect emotionally with the content, enhancing their engagement and retention. The visual and auditory elements of puppetry cater to various learning styles, ensuring that all students can find a way to connect with the material. In addition to cognitive benefits, puppetry also promotes social skills. Working collaboratively on puppet projects encourages teamwork, communication, and empathy. Students learn to listen to one another, share ideas, and negotiate roles, all of which are essential skills in both academic and real-world settings. The collaborative nature of puppetry fosters a sense of community within the classroom, creating an environment where students feel safe to express themselves and take risks. Furthermore, puppetry can be an effective tool for addressing sensitive topics. Whether discussing emotions, social issues, or historical events, puppets can provide a safe distance for students to explore difficult subjects. The playful nature of puppetry allows for open dialogue, enabling students to express their thoughts and feelings without fear of judgment. This can be particularly beneficial in diverse classrooms where students may come from varying backgrounds and experiences. In summary, the educational benefits of puppetry are extensive. By engaging students in a dynamic and interactive manner, puppetry fosters creativity, enhances storytelling, promotes social skills, and provides a safe space for exploring complex topics. As educators continue to seek innovative ways to engage their students, puppetry stands out as a versatile and impactful tool in the educational arsenal.

Creating Learning Characters

The creation of learning characters through puppetry is a delightful process that not only captivates students but also serves as a powerful pedagogical strategy. These characters can embody various traits, emotions, and experiences, allowing students to explore different perspectives and learn valuable lessons in a fun and engaging way. When designing learning characters, it is essential to consider the educational goals at hand. What concepts or skills do you want your students to grasp? Once these objectives are clear, the character creation process can begin. This involves brainstorming ideas, sketching designs, and developing backstories that align with the intended lessons. For instance, a puppet character designed to teach empathy might have a backstory that includes experiences of loss or friendship, allowing students to relate to the character on a personal level. The physical attributes of the puppet also play a crucial role in character creation. Colors, shapes, and materials can all convey specific messages and emotions. A bright, cheerful puppet might be used to teach positive reinforcement, while a more subdued character could be employed to discuss feelings of sadness or frustration. By carefully selecting these attributes, educators can create characters that resonate with students and enhance their learning experience. Once the characters are created, they can be integrated into various educational activities. For example, puppets can be used in role-playing scenarios, where students take on the roles of both the puppets and their creators. This interactive approach encourages students to think critically about the characters' motivations and actions, deepening their understanding of the subject matter. Additionally, students can create their own puppets, allowing them to express their creativity while reinforcing the lessons learned. The process of creating learning characters also fosters collaboration among students. Working together to design and develop puppets encourages teamwork and communication, as students must share ideas and negotiate roles. This collaborative spirit not only enhances the learning experience but also builds a sense of community within the classroom. Moreover, learning characters can be used to bridge cultural gaps and promote inclusivity. By creating puppets that represent diverse backgrounds and experiences, educators can foster discussions about identity, culture, and acceptance. This not only enriches the educational experience but also prepares students to navigate an increasingly diverse world.

Engaging Students

Engaging students in the learning process is a fundamental goal of education, and puppetry offers a unique avenue to achieve this. The dynamic nature of puppetry captures students' attention, making learning an enjoyable and memorable experience. By incorporating puppetry into the classroom, educators can create an environment that fosters curiosity, creativity, and active participation. One of the most effective ways to engage students through puppetry is by allowing them to take an active role in the puppet-making process. When students are involved in creating their own puppets, they develop a sense of ownership and pride in their work. This investment in the project encourages them to engage more deeply with the content, as they are not merely passive observers but active creators. The tactile experience of crafting puppets also appeals to kinesthetic learners, providing them with a hands-on approach to education. Once the puppets are created, they can be used in a variety of engaging activities. Puppet shows, for instance, allow students to showcase their characters and the stories they have developed. This not only reinforces the lessons learned but also provides an opportunity for public speaking and performance skills to flourish. The excitement of performing in front of peers can motivate students to put forth their best effort, leading to a deeper understanding of the material. Additionally, puppetry can be used to facilitate discussions and encourage critical thinking. By presenting scenarios through puppets, educators can prompt students to analyze situations, consider different perspectives, and engage in meaningful dialogue. For example, a puppet character facing a moral dilemma can spark discussions about ethics, empathy, and decision-making. This interactive approach encourages students to think critically and articulate their thoughts, enhancing their communication skills. Puppetry also lends itself well to interdisciplinary learning. Educators can integrate puppetry into various subjects, such as history, science, and language arts. For instance, students can create puppets representing historical figures and reenact significant events, bringing history to life in a way that textbooks cannot. This cross-curricular approach not only engages students but also helps them make connections between different subjects, fostering a holistic understanding of the material. Furthermore, the use of puppetry can cater to diverse learning styles and abilities. Visual learners benefit from the colorful and dynamic nature of puppets, while auditory learners engage with the dialogue and storytelling aspects. Kinesthetic learners thrive in the hands-on creation and manipulation of puppets. By incorporating puppetry into the classroom, educators can create an inclusive environment that meets the needs of all students. In summary, engaging students through puppetry is a powerful strategy that enhances the learning experience. By involving students in the puppet-making process, facilitating discussions, and integrating puppetry into various subjects, educators can create a vibrant and dynamic classroom environment. The joy and excitement that puppetry brings to education not only captivates students but also fosters a love for learning that can last a lifetime.

Chapter 26: Puppetry in Therapy

Therapeutic Benefits

Puppetry, a time-honored art form, transcends mere entertainment, emerging as a powerful therapeutic tool that fosters healing and emotional expression. The act of manipulating a puppet allows individuals to explore their feelings in a safe and controlled environment. This unique medium serves as a bridge between the conscious and subconscious, enabling participants to articulate thoughts and emotions that may otherwise remain unexpressed. The therapeutic benefits of puppetry are manifold. For children, puppets can serve as a non-threatening conduit for communication. Young ones often find it challenging to articulate their feelings directly, but when a puppet takes center stage, the barriers dissolve. They can project their fears, joys, and anxieties onto the puppet, allowing for a dialogue that feels less intimidating. This process not only aids in emotional expression but also cultivates empathy, as children learn to understand and relate to the experiences of others through their puppet characters. For adults, puppetry can be equally transformative. It offers a creative outlet for those grappling with trauma, grief, or mental health challenges. Engaging with puppets can facilitate a sense of playfulness and spontaneity, which is often lost in the seriousness of adult life. This playful engagement can unlock new perspectives on personal struggles, fostering resilience and healing. Moreover, puppetry can enhance social skills and improve interpersonal relationships. In group therapy settings, puppetry encourages collaboration and communication among participants. By working together to create stories and characters, individuals can build trust and camaraderie, essential components of the therapeutic process. The shared experience of puppetry can break down social barriers, allowing for deeper connections and understanding. The use of puppetry in therapy is not limited to traditional settings. It has found its way into schools, hospitals, and community centers, reaching diverse populations. From children with autism to elderly individuals facing cognitive decline, puppetry offers a versatile approach to healing that can be tailored to meet the unique needs of various groups.

Creating Healing Characters

The process of creating healing characters is an integral aspect of therapeutic puppetry. These characters are not merely puppets; they embody the emotions, experiences, and aspirations of the individuals they represent. When crafting a healing character, it is essential to consider the specific needs and challenges of the participant. This character becomes a vessel for exploration and understanding, allowing individuals to navigate their inner worlds. To begin, one must engage in a collaborative dialogue with the participant. This conversation should delve into their feelings, fears, and desires. What emotions do they wish to express? What challenges do they face? By understanding the participant's unique narrative, the therapist can guide them in designing a puppet that resonates with their experiences. The physical attributes of the puppet play a crucial role in its therapeutic potential. The choice of colors, textures, and shapes can evoke specific emotions and memories. For instance, a puppet adorned in bright colors may symbolize joy and positivity, while darker hues might represent sadness or fear. The design process becomes an artistic exploration, where the participant's emotions are translated into tangible form. Voice and movement are equally significant in the creation of healing characters. Participants are encouraged to experiment with different voices and gestures, allowing them to embody their puppet fully. This process can be liberating, as individuals step outside of themselves and explore different facets of their identity. The puppet becomes an extension of their own voice, enabling them to communicate in ways that feel authentic and empowering. As the character takes shape, it is essential to establish a backstory that reflects the participant's journey. This narrative can serve as a therapeutic tool, providing a framework for understanding and processing emotions. The puppet's experiences can mirror those of the participant, creating a sense of connection and validation. Through storytelling, individuals can gain insights into their struggles, fostering a sense of agency and empowerment. Ultimately, the creation of healing characters is a deeply personal and transformative process. It invites individuals to explore their emotions, confront their fears, and celebrate their strengths. The puppet becomes a trusted companion on their journey toward healing, offering solace and support in times of need.

Case Studies

One compelling case study involves a group of children diagnosed with autism spectrum disorder (ASD). In a therapeutic setting, a trained puppeteer introduced a series of puppet characters, each representing different emotions. The children were encouraged to interact with the puppets, expressing their feelings through play. Over several sessions, the children began to identify and articulate their emotions more effectively. The puppets served as a bridge, allowing them to communicate in a way that felt safe and engaging. As a result, the children demonstrated improved social skills and emotional awareness, showcasing the profound impact of puppetry in therapeutic contexts. Another case study highlights the use of puppetry in a hospital setting for children undergoing medical treatment. A team of therapists collaborated with puppeteers to create a puppet character named "Brave Benny," who faced similar medical challenges. Through storytelling and role-playing, children were able to express their fears about procedures and treatments. The puppet became a source of comfort and inspiration, encouraging children to embrace their bravery in the face of adversity. This innovative approach not only alleviated anxiety but also fostered a sense of community among the young patients, as they shared their experiences through the lens of the puppet. In a different context, a group of elderly individuals in a nursing home participated in a puppetry workshop designed to address feelings of isolation and loneliness. The participants were guided in creating their own puppet characters, reflecting their life stories and experiences. As they engaged in storytelling and performance, the residents found joy and connection in sharing their narratives. The puppets became vessels for reminiscence, allowing individuals to revisit cherished memories and foster relationships with one another. This case study illustrates the power of puppetry to bridge generational gaps and create meaningful connections among individuals facing similar challenges. These case studies exemplify the diverse applications of puppetry in therapeutic settings. Whether working with children, adults, or the elderly, puppetry offers a unique and effective means of fostering healing, communication, and connection. As the field of therapeutic puppetry continues to evolve, it holds immense potential for enriching the lives of individuals across various demographics, providing a creative outlet for expression and exploration.

Chapter 27: Exploring Different Genres

Puppetry, as an art form, transcends the boundaries of mere entertainment. It serves as a vessel for storytelling, a medium through which emotions are conveyed, and a canvas for the imagination. Each genre of puppetry offers unique opportunities for character creation, allowing puppeteers to explore diverse themes, styles, and narratives. In this chapter, we will delve into the various genres of puppetry, examining how they influence character development and the creative process.

Fantasy

The realm of fantasy is perhaps the most enchanting genre within the world of puppetry. It invites audiences to step into worlds where the impossible becomes possible, where mythical creatures roam, and where the laws of nature bend to the whims of imagination. In fantasy puppetry, characters often embody archetypes that resonate with universal themes of heroism, adventure, and the eternal struggle between good and evil. When creating characters for a fantasy puppet show, one must first consider the fantastical elements that will define their existence. Will your character be a brave knight, a cunning sorceress, or perhaps a whimsical creature from the depths of an enchanted forest? The physical attributes of these characters can be exaggerated to enhance their fantastical nature. For instance, a dragon puppet might feature vibrant colors, oversized wings, and intricate scales, while a fairy could be adorned with delicate, shimmering fabrics that evoke a sense of magic. The backstory of fantasy characters is equally important. Audiences are drawn to characters with rich histories and motivations. A puppet knight may have a tragic past that fuels their quest for redemption, while a mischievous sprite might be driven by a desire to prove their worth in a world that underestimates them. By crafting compelling backstories, puppeteers can create characters that resonate deeply with their audience, inviting them to invest emotionally in the unfolding narrative. Voice and speech patterns play a crucial role in bringing fantasy characters to life. The tone, pitch, and cadence of a character's voice can convey their personality and intentions. A wise old wizard might speak in a slow, deliberate manner, while a sprightly elf could have a light, airy voice that dances with excitement. By carefully considering how each character communicates, puppeteers can enhance the overall experience, making the fantastical world feel more immersive and engaging. Movement and expression are equally vital in fantasy puppetry. Characters often possess unique physical traits that influence how they move. A giant puppet may lumber across the stage with heavy, deliberate steps, while a nimble fairy flits about with grace and agility. The use of exaggerated movements can heighten the sense of wonder, allowing audiences to suspend their disbelief and fully embrace the magic of the performance. In the realm of fantasy, humor can also play a significant role. Comedic elements can be woven into the narrative, providing levity amidst the grand adventures. A bumbling wizard who constantly miscasts spells or a dragon with a penchant for puns can add a delightful layer of humor that resonates with audiences of all ages. By balancing humor with the more serious themes of fantasy, puppeteers can create a rich tapestry of storytelling that captivates and entertains.

Comedy

Comedy, as a genre, thrives on the unexpected, the absurd, and the delightful interplay of characters. Puppetry lends itself beautifully to comedic storytelling, allowing for exaggerated expressions, physical humor, and witty dialogue that can elicit laughter from audiences. In this genre, character creation is often centered around the quirks and idiosyncrasies that make each puppet unique and relatable. When developing comedic characters, it is essential to embrace the absurdity of their situations. A puppet might find themselves in a series of increasingly ridiculous predicaments, such as a clumsy chef who can't seem to get a recipe right or a hapless detective who misinterprets every clue. These characters often embody traits that amplify their comedic potential, such as overconfidence, naivety, or a penchant for slapstick humor. Physical attributes play a significant role in comedic puppetry. Characters can be designed with exaggerated features that enhance their comedic appeal. A puppet with an oversized head and tiny limbs can create a visual contrast that is inherently funny, while a character with an outlandishly large nose might find themselves in humorous situations that highlight their unique appearance. The visual design of comedic puppets should invite laughter even before they utter a word. Voice and speech patterns are equally important in comedy. The delivery of lines can make or break a comedic moment. A character with a high-pitched, squeaky voice can add an element of silliness, while a deep, booming voice can create a humorous juxtaposition when paired with a small puppet. Timing is crucial in comedy, and the rhythm of dialogue should be carefully crafted to maximize comedic effect. Pauses, inflections, and unexpected punchlines can elevate the humor and keep audiences engaged. Movement and expression are vital components of comedic puppetry. Characters often engage in exaggerated physicality, employing slapstick techniques that elicit laughter through visual gags. A puppet might trip over its own feet, engage in a comical chase, or perform absurd dance moves that defy logic. The ability to convey humor through movement allows puppeteers to create memorable moments that resonate with audiences long after the performance ends. In comedic puppetry, the interplay between characters can also drive the humor. Dynamic relationships, such as a straight man paired with a comedic foil, can create a delightful tension that fuels the comedic narrative. The banter between characters, filled with witty repartee and playful teasing, can enhance the overall comedic experience, inviting audiences to revel in the joy of laughter.

Drama

Dramatic puppetry offers a powerful avenue for exploring complex emotions, human experiences, and profound themes. In this genre, character creation takes on a more nuanced approach, as puppeteers strive to convey the depth of human emotion through their puppets. The characters in dramatic puppetry often grapple with internal conflicts, moral dilemmas, and the intricacies of relationships, inviting audiences to reflect on their own experiences. When developing characters for dramatic puppetry, it is essential to delve into their emotional landscapes. What drives them? What fears or desires shape their actions? A puppet character may embody the struggles of loss, love, or identity, allowing audiences to connect on a deeply personal level. By crafting rich backstories that reveal the character's motivations and vulnerabilities, puppeteers can create a sense of empathy that resonates with viewers. Physical attributes in dramatic puppetry can be designed to reflect the emotional state of the character. A puppet burdened by sorrow might have slumped shoulders and downcast eyes, while a character filled with hope could be portrayed with an upright posture and bright, expressive features. The visual design should serve as a reflection of the character's inner world, enhancing the emotional impact of the performance. Voice and speech patterns are crucial in conveying the emotional depth of dramatic characters. The tone of voice can evoke a range of feelings, from despair to joy. A character grappling with grief may speak in a hushed, trembling voice, while one experiencing newfound love might express themselves with exuberance. The subtleties of vocal delivery can elevate the emotional stakes, drawing audiences into the character's journey. Movement and expression play a significant role in dramatic puppetry. Characters often engage in nuanced gestures that convey their emotional states. A puppet might clutch its heart in anguish or extend its arms in a gesture of longing. The use of stillness can also be powerful; a moment of silence can speak volumes, allowing audiences to absorb the weight of the character's experience. By carefully choreographing movements, puppeteers can create a visual language that resonates with the emotional core of the narrative. In dramatic puppetry, the relationships between characters are often fraught with tension and complexity. The dynamics of love, betrayal, and reconciliation can be explored through the interactions of puppets, inviting audiences to witness the intricacies of human connection. By crafting compelling dialogues and moments of conflict, puppeteers can create a rich tapestry of storytelling that captivates and moves viewers.

And More

Beyond the realms of fantasy, comedy, and drama, puppetry encompasses a myriad of genres that invite exploration and innovation. Each genre offers unique opportunities for character creation, allowing puppeteers to experiment with different styles, themes, and narratives. From educational puppetry that imparts valuable lessons to avant-garde performances that challenge conventions, the possibilities are endless. In educational puppetry, characters are often designed to engage and inform young audiences. These puppets can embody relatable figures, such as friendly animals or wise mentors, who guide children through important lessons about friendship, empathy, and problem-solving. The character design should be approachable and visually appealing, capturing the attention of young viewers while conveying meaningful messages. Avant-garde puppetry pushes the boundaries of traditional storytelling, inviting audiences to engage with abstract concepts and unconventional narratives. Characters in this genre may defy categorization, taking on surreal forms and embodying complex ideas. The creative process in avant-garde puppetry often involves experimentation with materials, movement, and sound, resulting in a unique and thought-provoking experience for audiences. Puppetry can also intersect with various cultural traditions, allowing for the exploration of diverse narratives and character archetypes. Characters inspired by folklore, mythology, and cultural heritage can enrich the storytelling experience, offering audiences a glimpse into different perspectives and histories. By honoring these traditions, puppeteers can create characters that resonate with authenticity and depth. In the realm of social change, puppetry serves as a powerful tool for advocacy and awareness. Characters can be crafted to address pressing societal issues, such as environmental concerns, social justice, and mental health. By using puppetry as a medium for activism, puppeteers can engage audiences in meaningful conversations and inspire action through the lens of character-driven narratives. Ultimately, the exploration of different genres in puppetry opens up a world of possibilities for character creation. Each genre invites puppeteers to embrace their creativity, experiment with storytelling techniques, and connect with audiences on a profound level. Whether through the whimsical charm of fantasy, the laughter of comedy, the emotional depth of drama, or the innovative spirit of avant-garde puppetry, the art of character creation remains a vibrant and ever-evolving journey.

Chapter 28: The Evolution of Puppetry

Puppetry, an art form that transcends time and culture, has undergone a remarkable transformation throughout its history. From its ancient origins to its contemporary manifestations, the evolution of puppetry reflects broader societal changes, technological advancements, and artistic innovations. This chapter delves into the historical changes, modern innovations, and future trends that have shaped the world of puppetry.

Historical Changes

The roots of puppetry can be traced back thousands of years, with evidence of puppet-like figures found in ancient civilizations. The earliest known puppets date back to around 2000 BCE in Egypt, where they were used in religious ceremonies and storytelling. These early puppets were often made from simple materials like wood and cloth, manipulated by hand or strings. As civilizations evolved, so did the art of puppetry. In ancient Greece, puppetry became a form of entertainment, with marionettes and shadow puppets captivating audiences. The Greeks utilized puppetry to convey complex narratives, often integrating it with theater. This tradition continued through the Roman Empire, where puppetry was used to entertain the masses in public spaces. During the Middle Ages, puppetry experienced a decline in popularity, largely due to the rise of the church, which viewed it as a form of pagan entertainment. However, the Renaissance marked a resurgence of interest in the arts, including puppetry. The introduction of the commedia dell'arte in Italy brought forth a new wave of puppet characters, each with distinct personalities and traits. The 18th and 19th centuries saw the emergence of puppet theaters across Europe, with famous puppeteers like Jean-Baptiste Poquelin (Molière) and later, the renowned Punch and Judy shows in England. These performances often reflected societal issues, using humor and satire to engage audiences. The 20th century brought about significant changes in puppetry, particularly with the advent of television. Shows like "Sesame Street" and "The Muppet Show" revolutionized the medium, introducing puppetry to a global audience. These programs not only entertained but also educated, showcasing the versatility of puppetry as a storytelling tool.

Table 1: Key Historical Milestones in Puppetry

Time Period	Key Developments
2000 BCE	Earliest known puppets in Egypt
Ancient Greece	Puppetry integrated with theater
Middle Ages	Decline due to church influence
Renaissance	Resurgence with commedia dell'arte
18th-19th Century	Emergence of puppet theaters in Europe
20th Century	Television puppetry gains popularity

The evolution of puppetry has been marked by its ability to adapt to changing cultural landscapes. Each era has contributed unique styles and techniques, enriching the art form and expanding its reach.

Modern Innovations

In the contemporary landscape, puppetry has embraced modern innovations that have transformed the way puppets are created, performed, and experienced. The integration of technology has opened new avenues for puppeteers, allowing them to push the boundaries of traditional puppetry. One of the most significant advancements is the use of digital puppetry. This technique combines traditional puppetry with digital animation, enabling puppeteers to create characters that can be manipulated in real-time using motion capture technology. This fusion of art forms has led to groundbreaking performances that captivate audiences with their visual spectacle. Additionally, the rise of social media and online platforms has provided puppeteers with new opportunities to showcase their work. Platforms like YouTube and Instagram have given rise to a new generation of puppeteers who create content that resonates with diverse audiences. These digital puppeteers often blend humor, social commentary, and creativity, reflecting contemporary issues and trends. The use of puppetry in education has also gained traction in recent years. Educators have recognized the power of puppetry as a tool for engagement and learning. Puppets can help convey complex concepts, making them accessible to students of all ages. Workshops and programs that incorporate puppetry into curricula have emerged, fostering creativity and communication skills among learners.

Table 2: Modern Innovations in Puppetry

Innovation	Description
Digital Puppetry	Combines traditional puppetry with digital animation
Social Media Platforms	Allows puppeteers to reach global audiences
Puppetry in Education	Utilizes puppets as tools for learning and engagement

Moreover, the exploration of new materials and techniques has led to innovative puppet designs. Puppeteers are experimenting with sustainable materials, 3D printing, and mixed media to create unique characters that challenge conventional aesthetics. This creativity not only enhances the visual appeal of puppetry but also aligns with contemporary values of sustainability and environmental consciousness. The modern puppetry landscape is characterized by collaboration across disciplines. Puppeteers are increasingly working with visual artists, musicians, and filmmakers to create interdisciplinary performances that blur the lines between art forms. This collaborative spirit fosters a vibrant community of artists who share ideas and push the boundaries of what puppetry can achieve.

Future Trends

As we look to the future, the evolution of puppetry is poised to continue its dynamic trajectory. Several trends are emerging that will shape the next generation of puppetry, reflecting the changing cultural and technological landscape. One significant trend is the increasing focus on inclusivity and representation within puppetry. As audiences become more diverse, puppeteers are recognizing the importance of creating characters that reflect a wide range of experiences and identities. This shift towards inclusivity not only enriches the art form but also fosters a sense of belonging among audiences. The integration of augmented reality (AR) and virtual reality (VR) into puppetry is another exciting development on the horizon. These technologies have the potential to create immersive experiences that transport audiences into fantastical worlds where puppets come to life in unprecedented ways. Imagine attending a puppet show where characters interact with the audience in a virtual space, blurring the lines between reality and imagination. Furthermore, the global exchange of ideas and techniques is likely to continue shaping the future of puppetry. As artists from different cultures collaborate and share their practices, we can expect to see a rich tapestry of styles and narratives emerge. This cross-pollination of ideas will not only enhance the artistry of puppetry but also promote cultural understanding and appreciation.

Table 3: Future Trends in Puppetry

Trend	Description
Inclusivity and Representation	Creating diverse characters that reflect various identities
Augmented and Virtual Reality	Immersive experiences that enhance audience engagement
Global Collaboration	Exchange of ideas and techniques across cultures

In addition, the rise of environmental consciousness is likely to influence puppet design and production. Puppeteers may increasingly prioritize sustainable practices, using eco-friendly materials and methods to create their characters. This commitment to sustainability aligns with broader societal movements towards environmental responsibility, ensuring that puppetry remains relevant in a changing world. As the art of puppetry continues to evolve, it remains a powerful medium for storytelling, expression, and connection. The journey of puppetry is a testament to the resilience and creativity of artists who have embraced change while honoring tradition. The future holds exciting possibilities for puppetry, inviting new generations of puppeteers to explore, innovate, and inspire through this timeless art form.

Chapter 29: Creating Memorable Side Characters

Creating memorable side characters is an art form that enhances the tapestry of any puppetry performance. These characters, often overlooked, serve as the vibrant threads that weave together the narrative, providing depth, humor, and emotional resonance. In this chapter, we will explore the essential roles that side characters play, how they enhance main characters, and the ways in which they add depth to the overall story.

Supporting Roles

Side characters are the unsung heroes of puppetry. They support the protagonist's journey, often acting as confidants, comic relief, or even antagonists. Their presence is crucial in establishing the world in which the main character operates. A well-crafted side character can illuminate the protagonist's traits, motivations, and struggles, allowing the audience to connect more deeply with the central narrative. To create effective supporting roles, one must first understand the purpose of each character within the story. Consider the archetypes that can be employed: the mentor, the sidekick, the foil, or the love interest. Each of these roles serves a distinct function, contributing to the protagonist's development and the narrative's progression. For instance, the mentor character often embodies wisdom and experience, guiding the main character through challenges. This dynamic can be particularly poignant in puppetry, where the mentor's physicality and voice can contrast sharply with the youthful exuberance of the protagonist. The mentor's age and demeanor can add layers to the performance, allowing the audience to appreciate the wisdom imparted through dialogue and action. The sidekick, on the other hand, provides companionship and support, often injecting humor into the narrative. This character can be a source of levity, balancing the weight of the protagonist's journey. The interplay between the sidekick and the main character can create delightful moments of camaraderie, showcasing the importance of friendship and loyalty. Moreover, the foil character serves to highlight the protagonist's qualities by presenting contrasting traits. This juxtaposition can lead to moments of introspection for the main character, prompting growth and self-discovery. In puppetry, the physical differences between the protagonist and the foil can be exaggerated, enhancing the visual storytelling and making their interactions more engaging. When crafting supporting roles, it is essential to ensure that these characters are not mere caricatures or stereotypes. They should possess their own unique traits, motivations, and arcs. This complexity allows them to resonate with the audience, making their contributions to the story feel authentic and meaningful. Consider the character of a wise old owl who serves as a mentor to a young, impulsive bird. The owl's calm demeanor and thoughtful advice can provide a stark contrast to the young bird's eagerness, creating a dynamic that is both entertaining and enlightening. The audience can appreciate the wisdom of the owl while rooting for the young bird's growth, making both characters memorable in their own right.

Enhancing Main Characters

The relationship between side characters and main characters is a delicate dance that can elevate a puppetry performance to new heights. Side characters have the power to enhance the main character's journey, providing essential support, conflict, and perspective. Their interactions can reveal hidden facets of the protagonist, allowing the audience to see them in a new light. One of the most effective ways side characters enhance main characters is through dialogue. The conversations between these characters can reveal the protagonist's vulnerabilities, desires, and fears. For example, a loyal friend may challenge the main character's decisions, prompting them to reflect on their choices. This dynamic not only adds depth to the protagonist but also creates opportunities for character growth. In puppetry, the physicality of the characters can further amplify this enhancement. The contrasting movements and expressions of the side character can highlight the main character's emotional state. A timid puppet may shrink back in the presence of a boisterous sidekick, visually demonstrating their insecurities. This interplay of movement and expression enriches the storytelling, allowing the audience to engage with the characters on a deeper level. Moreover, side characters can serve as catalysts for change in the main character's arc. A character who embodies courage may inspire the protagonist to confront their fears, leading to a pivotal moment of transformation. This journey of self-discovery can resonate with the audience, making the main character's growth feel authentic and relatable. Consider a scenario where a shy puppet is paired with an outgoing side character. The side character's exuberance can encourage the shy puppet to step out of their comfort zone, leading to a series of humorous and heartwarming moments. As the shy puppet gains confidence, the audience witnesses their evolution, making the journey all the more impactful. In addition to dialogue and movement, the emotional connections between characters can enhance the main character's journey. A side character who shares a deep bond with the protagonist can evoke empathy from the audience, making their struggles feel more poignant. The audience becomes invested in the relationship, rooting for both characters as they navigate challenges together. Furthermore, side characters can introduce subplots that enrich the main narrative. These subplots can provide additional layers of complexity, allowing the audience to explore different themes and emotions. For instance, a side character's quest for love can parallel the main character's journey, creating a tapestry of interconnected stories that resonate with the audience. Ultimately, the interplay between side characters and main characters is a vital aspect of puppetry. By crafting nuanced relationships and allowing these characters to influence one another, puppeteers can create a rich and engaging narrative that captivates audiences of all ages.

Adding Depth

The depth of a puppetry performance is often determined by the richness of its characters, both main and side. Side characters, in particular, have the potential to add layers of complexity to the story, enhancing the emotional resonance and thematic depth of the narrative. By exploring the motivations, backgrounds, and relationships of these characters, puppeteers can create a more immersive experience for the audience. One way to add depth to side characters is through their backstories. Just as main characters benefit from a well-developed history, side characters can also have rich narratives that inform their actions and decisions. A character's past experiences can shape their personality, providing context for their behavior in the present. For example, a grumpy old puppet may have a backstory that reveals a history of loss or disappointment. Understanding this character's past can evoke empathy from the audience, transforming them from a mere comic foil into a multidimensional figure. This depth allows the audience to connect with the character on an emotional level, making their interactions with the main character more meaningful. In addition to backstories, the relationships between side characters and the main character can add depth to the narrative. The dynamics of friendship, rivalry, or mentorship can create a rich tapestry of interactions that resonate with the audience. These relationships can evolve throughout the story, reflecting the characters' growth and development. Consider a scenario where a side character initially serves as a rival to the main character. As the story progresses, their rivalry may transform into a friendship, showcasing the power of forgiveness and understanding. This evolution not only adds depth to both characters but also reinforces the overarching themes of the narrative. Furthermore, side characters can introduce new perspectives that challenge the main character's worldview. A character with a contrasting belief system can prompt the protagonist to question their assumptions, leading to moments of introspection and growth. This exploration of differing viewpoints enriches the narrative, allowing the audience to engage with complex themes and ideas. The physicality of side characters can also contribute to their depth. The design and movement of these characters can reflect their personalities and experiences. A character who is timid may have hunched shoulders and slow movements, while a bold character may exude confidence through their posture and gestures. These visual cues enhance the storytelling, allowing the audience to glean insights into the characters' inner lives. Moreover, the emotional range of side characters can add depth to the overall performance. Characters who experience joy, sorrow, anger, or fear can evoke a spectrum of emotions in the audience. By showcasing the emotional journeys of side characters, puppeteers can create a more immersive experience, inviting the audience to empathize with the characters' struggles and triumphs.

Chapter 30: The Art of Improvisation

Spontaneity in Performance

Improvisation in puppetry is akin to a dance where the puppeteer and puppet become one, moving fluidly through a landscape of creativity and spontaneity. The essence of improvisation lies in the ability to respond to the unexpected, to embrace the moment, and to allow the character to breathe and evolve in real-time. This dynamic interplay transforms a scripted performance into a living, breathing entity, captivating audiences with its authenticity and unpredictability. At its core, spontaneity in performance invites a sense of playfulness. Puppeteers must cultivate an environment where both they and their puppets can explore the boundaries of their characters. This requires a deep understanding of the puppet's personality, motivations, and quirks. When a puppeteer is attuned to their character, they can navigate the uncharted waters of improvisation with confidence and grace. Consider the scenario of a live performance where an unexpected event occurs—perhaps a child in the audience shouts a question or a prop malfunctions. In these moments, the puppeteer has the opportunity to weave the unexpected into the fabric of the performance. The character can respond with wit, humor, or even vulnerability, creating a connection with the audience that scripted lines may not achieve. This spontaneity not only entertains but also fosters a sense of community, as the audience becomes part of the unfolding narrative. To master spontaneity, puppeteers can engage in exercises that enhance their improvisational skills. One effective technique is to practice "yes, and…" scenarios, where the puppeteer builds upon an idea introduced by their puppet or fellow performers. This approach encourages collaboration and creativity, allowing characters to evolve organically. Additionally, puppeteers can benefit from improvisational games that challenge them to think on their feet, respond to cues, and embrace the unexpected. The beauty of spontaneity in puppetry lies in its ability to surprise both the audience and the puppeteer. Each performance becomes a unique experience, a tapestry woven from the threads of creativity, humor, and emotion. As puppeteers embrace the art of improvisation, they unlock new dimensions of their characters, allowing them to resonate deeply with audiences and leave lasting impressions.

Character Flexibility

Character flexibility is a vital component of successful improvisation in puppetry. It refers to the ability of a puppet character to adapt and transform in response to the unfolding narrative and the audience's reactions. This flexibility not only enhances the performance but also enriches the character's depth, making them more relatable and engaging. A flexible character can navigate various emotional landscapes, shifting from joy to sorrow, from anger to compassion, often within the span of a single performance. This fluidity allows the puppeteer to explore the full spectrum of human experience, creating a rich tapestry of emotions that resonates with the audience. For instance, a puppet that begins as a comedic figure may find itself in a poignant moment, revealing layers of vulnerability that surprise and move the audience. To cultivate character flexibility, puppeteers must first establish a strong foundation for their characters. This involves understanding the character's core traits, motivations, and relationships. Once this foundation is set, the puppeteer can experiment with different emotional responses and scenarios, allowing the character to evolve organically. This process often involves improvisational exercises that encourage the puppeteer to step outside their comfort zone and explore new dimensions of their character. One effective method for enhancing character flexibility is through role-playing exercises. Puppeteers can engage in scenes where their characters are placed in unexpected situations, prompting them to react authentically. This practice not only sharpens the puppeteer's improvisational skills but also deepens their understanding of the character's psyche. As the puppeteer navigates these scenarios, they may discover new facets of the character that enrich the overall performance. Moreover, character flexibility extends beyond emotional responses; it also encompasses physicality. A puppet's movement can convey a wealth of information about its state of mind. A character that is anxious may fidget or shrink away, while one that is confident may stand tall and move boldly. By experimenting with different physical expressions, puppeteers can further enhance their character's flexibility, allowing them to respond dynamically to the performance environment. Ultimately, character flexibility is about embracing the journey of discovery. As puppeteers allow their characters to evolve in real-time, they create a vibrant and engaging experience for the audience. This adaptability not only enriches the performance but also fosters a deeper connection between the puppeteer, the puppet, and the audience, transforming each show into a unique and memorable event.

Audience Interaction

Audience interaction is a cornerstone of improvisational puppetry, transforming a performance into a shared experience that transcends the traditional boundaries between performer and spectator. Engaging with the audience not only enhances the spontaneity of the performance but also fosters a sense of community and connection, making each show a unique event. The art of audience interaction begins with the puppeteer's ability to read the room. Understanding the audience's energy, reactions, and engagement levels allows the puppeteer to tailor their performance accordingly. A responsive puppeteer can shift the tone, pace, and content of the performance based on the audience's cues, creating a dynamic interplay that keeps everyone invested in the unfolding story. One effective technique for fostering audience interaction is the use of direct address. When a puppet speaks directly to the audience, it breaks the fourth wall, inviting spectators to become active participants in the narrative. This approach can elicit laughter, surprise, and even emotional responses, as audience members feel a personal connection to the characters on stage. For instance, a puppet might ask a question or seek advice from the audience, creating an engaging dialogue that enhances the overall experience. In addition to direct address, puppeteers can incorporate interactive elements into their performances. This might involve inviting audience members on stage, encouraging them to participate in a scene, or even allowing them to influence the direction of the story. Such interactions not only create memorable moments but also empower the audience, making them feel like integral parts of the performance. Moreover, audience interaction can serve as a powerful tool for improvisation. When spectators respond with laughter, applause, or even unexpected comments, the puppeteer can adapt their performance in real-time, weaving these elements into the narrative. This responsiveness not only showcases the puppeteer's improvisational skills but also reinforces the idea that the performance is a collaborative effort between the puppeteer, the puppet, and the audience. To cultivate effective audience interaction, puppeteers can engage in exercises that enhance their ability to connect with spectators. This might include practicing improvisational games that focus on audience engagement or developing strategies for reading audience reactions. By honing these skills, puppeteers can create a more immersive and interactive experience, inviting audiences to become active participants in the storytelling process. Ultimately, audience interaction is about creating a shared experience that transcends the stage. As puppeteers embrace the art of improvisation and engage with their spectators, they foster a sense of community and connection that enriches the performance. This dynamic interplay not only captivates audiences but also transforms each show into a unique celebration of creativity, spontaneity, and collaboration.

Chapter 31: Puppetry in Film and Television

Adapting Characters

In the realm of film and television, the art of puppetry transcends mere performance; it becomes a vital conduit for storytelling, allowing characters to leap from the confines of imagination into the hearts of audiences. Adapting puppet characters for these mediums requires a nuanced understanding of both the original character's essence and the unique demands of screen storytelling. When adapting a puppet character for film or television, one must first consider the character's core attributes. What makes this character resonate with audiences? Is it their humor, their wisdom, or perhaps their vulnerability? The essence of the character must remain intact, even as the medium shifts. This often involves a deep dive into the character's backstory, motivations, and relationships, ensuring that they can navigate the new narrative landscape without losing their original charm. Moreover, the visual language of film and television presents an opportunity to enhance character traits through cinematography and editing. For instance, a puppet character known for their clumsiness can be portrayed with exaggerated physical comedy through clever camera angles and timing. The use of close-ups can capture the subtleties of a puppet's facial expressions, allowing for a deeper emotional connection with the audience. In addition to visual storytelling, sound design plays a crucial role in character adaptation. The voice of a puppet character can be reimagined to suit the tone of the film or show. A character that may have been portrayed with a whimsical tone in live performances might take on a more serious or nuanced voice in a cinematic context. This transformation can add layers to the character, making them more relatable and complex. The collaborative nature of film and television also allows for the integration of various artistic disciplines. Puppeteers, writers, directors, and animators must work in harmony to breathe life into the character. This collaboration can lead to innovative interpretations that enrich the character's narrative arc, making them more compelling to the audience. Ultimately, adapting puppet characters for film and television is a delicate balance of honoring the original creation while embracing the possibilities of the new medium. It is a journey that requires creativity, flexibility, and a deep understanding of the character's essence, ensuring that they continue to resonate with audiences in fresh and exciting ways.

Behind-the-Scenes

The magic of puppetry in film and television often lies behind the scenes, where a dedicated team of artists, technicians, and visionaries work tirelessly to bring puppet characters to life. This collaborative effort is a testament to the intricate craftsmanship that underpins the art of puppetry, revealing the layers of creativity that contribute to the final product. At the heart of this process is the puppeteer, whose skill and artistry are paramount. The puppeteer must not only master the mechanics of the puppet but also embody the character's personality, emotions, and intentions. This requires extensive rehearsal and a deep understanding of the character's nuances. In film and television, where timing and precision are crucial, puppeteers often work closely with directors to ensure that their performances align with the overall vision of the project. The design and construction of puppet characters are equally vital. Artisans and designers collaborate to create puppets that are visually striking and functional. This involves selecting materials that not only suit the character's aesthetic but also allow for the necessary range of motion. For instance, a puppet intended for action sequences may require a more robust design, while a character focused on subtle emotional expressions might benefit from a more delicate construction. In addition to the physical aspects, the integration of technology has revolutionized puppetry in film and television. The use of animatronics, motion capture, and digital effects has expanded the possibilities for character expression and interaction. Puppeteers can now work alongside animators to create hybrid characters that blend traditional puppetry with cutting-edge technology, resulting in a seamless fusion of artistry and innovation. Sound design and music also play a crucial role in the behind-the-scenes process. Voice actors lend their talents to bring puppet characters to life, often collaborating with the puppeteers to ensure that the vocal performance aligns with the physicality of the puppet. This synergy enhances the character's authenticity and emotional depth, allowing audiences to connect with them on a profound level. The behind-the-scenes world of puppetry in film and television is a vibrant tapestry of creativity, collaboration, and innovation. Each member of the team contributes their unique skills and perspectives, working together to craft unforgettable puppet characters that captivate audiences and leave a lasting impression.

Iconic Puppet Characters

Throughout the history of film and television, certain puppet characters have transcended their medium to become cultural icons. These characters, with their distinct personalities and memorable traits, have left an indelible mark on popular culture, showcasing the power of puppetry to resonate with audiences of all ages. One of the most beloved puppet characters is Kermit the Frog, created by Jim Henson. Kermit embodies a unique blend of optimism, humor, and relatability. His iconic catchphrase, "Hi-ho, Kermit the Frog here!" has become synonymous with his character, inviting audiences into his world. Kermit's adventures on "The Muppet Show" and in various films have showcased his ability to navigate challenges with grace and wit, making him a timeless figure in the realm of puppetry. Another iconic character is Elmo, also from the Muppet universe. With his bright red fur and childlike innocence, Elmo has captured the hearts of children and adults alike. His inquisitive nature and playful spirit make him a perfect ambassador for early childhood education, as seen in his role on "Sesame Street." Elmo's ability to address complex topics in a simple and engaging manner has solidified his status as a beloved character in educational programming. In the realm of television, the character of Mr. Snuffleupagus from "Sesame Street" stands out as a symbol of friendship and understanding. Initially perceived as an imaginary friend, Snuffy's eventual reveal to the adult characters on the show highlighted the importance of believing in the unseen and embracing the whimsical aspects of childhood. His gentle demeanor and heartfelt interactions with other characters have made him a cherished figure in the hearts of viewers. The artistry of puppetry is not limited to the Muppets; characters like the Cookie Monster have also made a significant impact. With his insatiable appetite for cookies and his humorous antics, the Cookie Monster embodies the joy of indulgence and the importance of moderation. His memorable catchphrases and comedic timing have made him a staple of children's programming, teaching valuable lessons while entertaining audiences. Beyond the Muppet universe, characters like the puppets from "Puppet Master" have carved a niche in the horror genre. These characters, often imbued with dark humor and sinister motives, showcase the versatility of puppetry in evoking a range of emotions. The juxtaposition of innocence and horror in these puppet characters adds a layer of complexity to their narratives, challenging audiences to confront their fears while engaging with the art form. The legacy of iconic puppet characters continues to inspire new generations of puppeteers and storytellers. Their ability to connect with audiences on an emotional level demonstrates the timeless appeal of puppetry as a medium for expression. As new characters emerge and old favorites are reimagined, the art of puppetry remains a vibrant and essential part of the storytelling landscape, inviting audiences to explore the depths of imagination and creativity.

Chapter 32: The Role of Puppetry in Storytelling

Puppetry, an ancient art form, has long been a vessel for storytelling, weaving narratives that resonate across cultures and generations. The unique ability of puppets to embody characters and convey emotions allows them to transcend mere entertainment, becoming powerful tools for storytelling. In this chapter, we will explore the intricate relationship between puppetry and storytelling through various narrative techniques, character arcs, and thematic elements.

Narrative Techniques

The narrative techniques employed in puppetry are as diverse as the puppets themselves. From traditional folk tales to contemporary narratives, puppetry offers a rich tapestry of storytelling methods that engage audiences on multiple levels.

1. Visual Storytelling

Puppetry is inherently visual, relying on the manipulation of characters to convey emotions and actions. The visual aspect of puppetry allows for a unique form of storytelling where the audience's imagination is sparked by the movements and expressions of the puppets.

Technique	Description
Body Language	Puppets communicate emotions through their physical movements, allowing for nuanced storytelling without spoken words.
Facial Expressions	Expressions crafted on puppet faces can convey a range of emotions, enhancing the narrative depth.
Staging and Set Design	The environment in which puppets perform can significantly impact the storytelling, adding layers of meaning and context.

2. Dialogue and Voice

The spoken word is a powerful narrative tool in puppetry. The voices of puppets, often distinct and memorable, contribute to character development and plot progression.

Element	Impact on Storytelling
Character Voices	Unique vocal traits help define characters, making them relatable and memorable.
Dialogue Delivery	The rhythm and pace of dialogue can create tension, humor, or emotional resonance.
Sound Effects	Incorporating sound effects can enhance the storytelling experience, immersing the audience in the narrative world.

3. Symbolism and Metaphor

Puppetry often employs symbolism and metaphor to convey deeper meanings. Puppets can represent various aspects of human experience, allowing for complex narratives that resonate on multiple levels.

Symbol	Meaning
Animal Puppets	Often symbolize human traits, such as cunning, loyalty, or bravery.
Color Choices	Colors can evoke specific emotions or themes, influencing audience perception.
Props	Objects used by puppets can symbolize larger concepts, such as power, love, or conflict.

Character Arcs

Character arcs are essential to storytelling, providing a framework for character development and transformation. In puppetry, the journey of a puppet character can mirror the complexities of human experience, allowing audiences to connect with the narrative on a personal level.

1. The Hero's Journey

Many puppet stories follow the classic hero's journey, where the protagonist faces challenges, undergoes transformation, and ultimately achieves growth. This archetypal structure resonates with audiences, as it reflects universal themes of struggle and triumph.

2. Transformation and Growth

Puppet characters often undergo significant transformations throughout the narrative. This growth can be physical, emotional, or moral, allowing audiences to witness the evolution of the character in a tangible way.

Stage	Description
Call to Adventure	The character is presented with a challenge that disrupts their ordinary world.
Trials and Tribulations	The character faces obstacles that test their resolve and character.
Climax	The character confronts their greatest challenge, leading to a moment of revelation.
Return	The character returns to their world, transformed by their experiences.

3. Relatable Flaws

Puppet characters often possess relatable flaws that make them more human. These imperfections allow audiences to empathize with their struggles and celebrate their victories.

Flaw	Character Example
Fear of Failure	A timid puppet who learns to embrace challenges.
Overconfidence	A boastful puppet who must learn humility.
Isolation	A puppet who struggles to connect with others but ultimately finds friendship.

Thematic Elements

Thematic elements in puppetry enrich storytelling, providing depth and resonance to the narratives. Themes can range from love and friendship to social justice and environmental awareness, allowing puppetry to address complex issues in an accessible manner.

1. Social Commentary

Puppetry has a long history of addressing social issues through satire and humor. By using puppets to represent societal problems, artists can engage audiences in critical conversations while entertaining them.

Theme	Example
Environmental Awareness	Puppets representing nature advocate for conservation and sustainability.
Equality and Justice	Puppets challenge stereotypes and promote inclusivity.
Community and Belonging	Puppets explore the importance of connection and support within communities.

2. The Power of Imagination

Puppetry celebrates the power of imagination, inviting audiences to explore fantastical worlds and characters. This theme encourages creativity and wonder, inspiring individuals to embrace their own imaginative potential.

3. The Human Experience

At its core, puppetry often reflects the complexities of the human experience. Themes of love, loss, joy, and sorrow resonate deeply with audiences, allowing them to see themselves in the stories being told.

Theme	Example
Love and Friendship	Puppets navigate relationships, highlighting the importance of connection.
Overcoming Adversity	Puppets face challenges that mirror real-life struggles, inspiring resilience.
Identity and Self-Discovery	Puppets embark on journeys of self-exploration, encouraging audiences to reflect on their own identities.

Chapter 33: Building a Puppet Character Portfolio

Documenting Characters

Creating a puppet character portfolio is an essential step for any puppeteer seeking to showcase their artistry and creativity. This portfolio serves not only as a collection of your work but also as a narrative that encapsulates the essence of each character you have brought to life. Documenting your characters involves a meticulous process of capturing their visual, emotional, and narrative elements, allowing potential collaborators, audiences, and clients to appreciate the depth and breadth of your creations.

To begin, consider the various aspects that define your puppet characters. Each character should be documented with a focus on their unique traits, backstory, and the artistic choices that influenced their design. This can be achieved through a combination of written descriptions, visual representations, and performance notes.

Character Profiles

A character profile is a comprehensive overview that includes the following elements:

- Name: The name of the character, which often reflects their personality or role in the story.

- Age: The character's age can influence their behavior, speech, and interactions with others.

- Physical Description: A detailed account of the character's appearance, including height, build, color scheme, and distinctive features.

- Personality Traits: A list of key traits that define the character, such as being cheerful, mischievous, or wise.

- Backstory: A brief narrative that explains the character's history, motivations, and relationships with other characters.

- Voice and Speech Patterns: Notes on how the character speaks, including accent, tone, and any unique phrases they might use.

This information can be organized in a table format for clarity:

Element	Description
Name	Charlie the Cheerful Clown
Age	30
Physical Description	Bright red hair, oversized shoes, colorful polka-dot costume
Personality Traits	Cheerful, playful, slightly clumsy
Backstory	Once a shy child, Charlie discovered the joy of making others laugh and became a clown.
Voice and Speech Patterns	High-pitched voice, often uses rhymes and jokes

This structured approach not only helps you keep track of your characters but also provides a clear and engaging way to present them to others.

Visual Documentation

In addition to written profiles, visual documentation is crucial for a puppet character portfolio. High-quality photographs or illustrations of your puppets in various poses and settings can vividly convey their personality and charm. Consider the following tips for effective visual documentation:

- Lighting: Use natural light or soft artificial lighting to highlight the puppet's features without harsh shadows.

- Background: Choose a neutral or thematic background that complements the character without distracting from it.

- Action Shots: Capture your puppets in action, whether during rehearsals or performances, to showcase their movement and expression.

- Close-Ups: Include close-up shots that focus on intricate details, such as facial expressions, costume elements, and textures.

Performance Notes

Performance notes are an invaluable addition to your character documentation. These notes can include insights into how the character is portrayed during performances, including:

- Movement Style: Describe the character's unique way of moving, whether it's graceful, erratic, or exaggerated.

- Interaction with Other Characters: Note how the character interacts with others, including their relationships and dynamics.

- Audience Engagement: Reflect on how the character connects with the audience, including any recurring themes or messages.

By combining written profiles, visual documentation, and performance notes, you create a rich tapestry that encapsulates the essence of each puppet character, making your portfolio a compelling showcase of your artistry.

Showcasing Skills

A puppet character portfolio is not merely a collection of characters; it is also a testament to your skills as a puppeteer and a storyteller. Showcasing your skills effectively can open doors to new opportunities, collaborations, and audiences. Here are several strategies to ensure your portfolio reflects your talents and creativity.

Highlighting Craftsmanship

One of the most important aspects of puppetry is the craftsmanship involved in creating the puppets themselves. Your portfolio should include examples of your work that demonstrate your skills in puppet construction, design, and manipulation. Consider the following elements:

- Puppet Construction: Include photographs or videos of the puppet-making process, showcasing the materials used, techniques applied, and the final product.

- Design Variations: If you have created multiple versions of a character or experimented with different designs, document these variations to illustrate your versatility.

- Manipulation Techniques: Provide video clips or descriptions of your manipulation techniques, highlighting your ability to bring characters to life through movement and expression.

Performance Highlights

Performance is at the heart of puppetry, and showcasing your skills in this area is essential. Include recordings of your performances, whether live or rehearsed, to demonstrate your ability to engage an audience. Consider the following tips:

- Diverse Repertoire: Feature a range of performances that showcase different styles, genres, and themes. This diversity will illustrate your adaptability and creativity as a puppeteer.

- Audience Reactions: If possible, include testimonials or feedback from audience members to highlight the impact of your performances.

- Collaboration with Other Artists: Document any collaborations with other puppeteers, actors, or musicians, showcasing your ability to work as part of a creative team.

Workshops and Teaching

If you have experience leading workshops or teaching puppetry, this is an excellent opportunity to showcase your skills. Include details about the workshops you have conducted, the topics covered, and any feedback received from participants. This not only demonstrates your expertise but also your commitment to sharing the art of puppetry with others.

Professional Presentation

The presentation of your puppet character portfolio is just as important as the content within it. A well-organized and visually appealing portfolio can leave a lasting impression on potential collaborators, clients, and audiences. Here are some key considerations for professional presentation.

Portfolio Format

Decide on the format of your portfolio based on your target audience and the context in which you will present it. Options include:

- Digital Portfolio: A website or PDF document that can be easily shared and accessed online. This format allows for multimedia elements, such as videos and interactive content.

- Physical Portfolio: A printed collection of photographs, character profiles, and performance notes. This format can be particularly impactful during in-person meetings or auditions.

Regardless of the format, ensure that your portfolio is well-organized and easy to navigate. Use clear headings, consistent fonts, and a cohesive color scheme to create a polished look.

Branding and Identity

Your portfolio should reflect your unique artistic identity as a puppeteer. Consider incorporating elements of your personal brand, such as a logo, color palette, and typography, to create a cohesive visual identity. This branding will help you stand out and make your portfolio memorable.

Regular Updates

As you continue to create new characters and develop your skills, it is essential to keep your portfolio updated. Regularly review and refresh your content to ensure it accurately reflects your current work and abilities. This not only keeps your portfolio relevant but also demonstrates your growth as an artist.

Chapter 34: The Psychology of Character Creation

Understanding Audience Perception

The intricate dance between puppeteer and audience is a delicate one, steeped in the nuances of perception and expectation. When crafting a puppet character, it is essential to consider how the audience will interpret and engage with the character. This understanding begins with recognizing that each viewer brings their own experiences, biases, and emotions to the performance. The puppeteer must navigate this landscape, creating characters that resonate on multiple levels. At the core of audience perception lies the concept of empathy. A well-crafted puppet character can evoke feelings of joy, sadness, anger, or nostalgia, depending on how effectively the puppeteer communicates the character's emotions. This emotional connection is often facilitated through visual cues, such as facial expressions and body language, as well as auditory elements, including voice modulation and sound effects. The puppeteer must be acutely aware of these elements, ensuring that they align with the character's intended persona. Moreover, the cultural context in which the audience exists plays a significant role in shaping their perception. Different cultures may interpret character traits and behaviors in varied ways. For instance, a character designed to be humorous in one culture may be perceived as offensive in another. Therefore, it is crucial for the puppeteer to conduct thorough research and engage with diverse perspectives when developing characters intended for a broader audience. The setting of the performance also influences audience perception. A puppet show staged in a cozy, intimate theater will elicit a different response than one performed in a large, open space. The atmosphere, lighting, and even the seating arrangement can affect how the audience connects with the characters. A puppeteer must adapt their performance style to suit the environment, ensuring that the character's traits are amplified or subdued as necessary. Ultimately, understanding audience perception is about creating a shared experience. The puppeteer must strive to build a bridge between the character and the viewers, allowing them to see parts of themselves reflected in the puppet. This connection fosters a deeper engagement, transforming a simple performance into a memorable experience that lingers long after the curtain falls.

Character Relatability

Relatability is a cornerstone of effective character creation in puppetry. When audiences can see themselves in a character, they are more likely to invest emotionally in the narrative. This connection can be achieved through various means, including the character's struggles, aspirations, and personality traits. The puppeteer must delve into the human experience, drawing upon universal themes that resonate across demographics. One effective approach to enhancing relatability is to incorporate flaws and vulnerabilities into the character's design. Perfection can be off-putting; audiences often gravitate toward characters who exhibit human-like imperfections. A puppet that stumbles, misjudges a situation, or grapples with self-doubt becomes more relatable, as these traits mirror the complexities of real life. By showcasing a character's journey through challenges, the puppeteer invites the audience to empathize with their plight, fostering a sense of connection. Furthermore, dialogue plays a pivotal role in establishing relatability. The language a character uses, their speech patterns, and even their humor can significantly impact how audiences perceive them. A character that speaks in a way that resonates with the audience's own experiences or cultural references can create an immediate bond. The puppeteer must be mindful of the character's voice, ensuring it aligns with their personality and the context of the story. In addition to dialogue, the character's relationships with others can enhance relatability. Characters that interact with a diverse cast, showcasing friendships, rivalries, or familial bonds, allow audiences to see reflections of their own relationships. These dynamics can evoke laughter, tears, or nostalgia, deepening the audience's emotional investment in the character's journey. Ultimately, relatability is about authenticity. The puppeteer must strive to create characters that feel genuine, reflecting the complexities of human nature. By tapping into shared experiences and emotions, the puppeteer can craft characters that resonate with audiences, transforming them into beloved figures that linger in the hearts and minds of viewers long after the performance concludes.

Psychological Depth

The psychological depth of a puppet character is what elevates them from mere objects of entertainment to profound representations of the human experience. To create a character with psychological depth, the puppeteer must explore the intricacies of human behavior, motivations, and emotions. This exploration involves delving into the character's psyche, understanding their desires, fears, and internal conflicts. One of the key elements of psychological depth is the character's backstory. A well-developed backstory provides context for the character's actions and decisions, allowing the audience to understand their motivations on a deeper level. The puppeteer should consider questions such as: What events shaped this character's life? What traumas or triumphs have they experienced? How do these experiences influence their current behavior? By answering these questions, the puppeteer can create a multi-dimensional character that resonates with audiences. Moreover, the character's emotional landscape is crucial in establishing psychological depth. Characters that experience a range of emotions—joy, sorrow, anger, and fear—become more relatable and engaging. The puppeteer must skillfully convey these emotions through the puppet's movements, expressions, and vocalizations. A character that can express vulnerability, for instance, invites the audience to empathize with their struggles, fostering a deeper connection. Another important aspect of psychological depth is the character's relationships with others. The dynamics between characters can reveal much about their personalities and motivations. A character that struggles with trust may exhibit defensive behavior, while one that seeks validation may go to great lengths to please others. By exploring these relationships, the puppeteer can create a rich tapestry of interactions that adds layers to the character's psychological profile. Additionally, the use of symbolism can enhance the psychological depth of a puppet character. Symbols can represent the character's inner conflicts, desires, or fears, providing the audience with visual cues that deepen their understanding. For example, a puppet that carries a broken mirror may symbolize the character's fractured self-image, inviting viewers to reflect on their own insecurities.

Chapter 35: Engaging with the Puppetry Community

The world of puppetry is a vibrant tapestry woven from the threads of creativity, collaboration, and community. Engaging with fellow puppeteers, artists, and enthusiasts can enrich your practice, inspire new ideas, and foster a sense of belonging. This chapter delves into the various ways you can immerse yourself in the puppetry community, exploring networking opportunities, collaborative projects, and avenues for continuous learning.

Networking

Networking within the puppetry community is not merely about exchanging business cards or making connections for future projects; it is about building relationships that can lead to artistic growth and innovation. The puppetry community is filled with diverse voices, each contributing unique perspectives and skills. By engaging with others, you can expand your horizons and discover new possibilities for your work. One of the most effective ways to network is to attend puppetry festivals and conventions. These gatherings bring together puppeteers from all over the world, offering a platform for sharing ideas, showcasing performances, and discussing the latest trends in the field. Events such as the National Puppetry Festival or the International Puppet Festival provide opportunities to meet established artists, emerging talents, and passionate enthusiasts. Engaging in workshops, panel discussions, and informal gatherings can lead to meaningful connections that may blossom into collaborations or mentorships. Social media has also transformed the way puppeteers connect. Platforms like Instagram, Facebook, and Twitter allow artists to share their work, seek feedback, and engage in conversations with a global audience. Joining online groups dedicated to puppetry can facilitate discussions about techniques, character development, and industry news. By actively participating in these communities, you can establish your presence and connect with like-minded individuals who share your passion for puppetry. Additionally, consider reaching out to local puppetry organizations or theaters. Many cities have puppetry groups that host events, workshops, and performances. Volunteering your time or skills can help you forge connections with seasoned puppeteers and gain insights into the local puppetry scene.

These grassroots efforts often lead to collaborative projects and can provide a supportive environment for honing your craft. Networking is not solely about personal gain; it is also about giving back to the community. By sharing your knowledge and experiences, you contribute to the collective growth of the puppetry world. Mentoring emerging artists, offering workshops, or participating in community outreach programs can create a ripple effect, inspiring others and fostering a culture of collaboration and support.

Collaborations

Collaboration is at the heart of puppetry, where the blending of ideas and talents can lead to extraordinary creations. Working with other artists—whether they are puppeteers, writers, musicians, or visual artists—can elevate your work and introduce new dimensions to your characters and performances. When embarking on a collaborative project, it is essential to establish clear communication and shared goals. Begin by discussing your vision for the project and how each participant can contribute their unique skills. This collaborative spirit encourages creativity and allows for the exploration of innovative ideas that may not have emerged in isolation. Consider partnering with writers to develop compelling narratives for your puppet characters. A well-crafted story can breathe life into your puppets, giving them depth and purpose. Collaborating with musicians can enhance the emotional resonance of your performances, as music can evoke feelings and set the tone for your characters' journeys. Visual artists can contribute to the design of puppets and sets, creating a cohesive aesthetic that captivates audiences. One inspiring example of collaboration in puppetry is the work of the renowned company, Handspring Puppet Company. Their innovative productions, such as "War Horse," showcase the seamless integration of puppetry, storytelling, and live performance. By collaborating with playwrights, directors, and designers, they create immersive experiences that resonate with audiences on multiple levels. This approach exemplifies how collaboration can lead to groundbreaking work that pushes the boundaries of traditional puppetry. Moreover, consider collaborating with artists from different disciplines. The intersection of puppetry with dance, theater, or visual arts can yield unexpected and exciting results. For instance, a puppetry performance that incorporates elements of contemporary dance can create a dynamic interplay between movement and storytelling, captivating audiences in new ways. Engaging in collaborative projects also fosters a sense of community and camaraderie among artists. The shared experience of creating something together can lead to lasting friendships and professional relationships. As you navigate the challenges and triumphs of collaboration, you will learn from one another, grow as an artist, and contribute to a vibrant artistic ecosystem.

Learning Opportunities

The journey of a puppeteer is one of continuous learning and exploration. Engaging with the puppetry community opens up a wealth of learning opportunities that can enhance your skills and deepen your understanding of the art form. Workshops and masterclasses are invaluable resources for aspiring puppeteers. Many festivals and organizations offer hands-on training sessions led by experienced artists. These workshops cover a wide range of topics, from puppet construction and manipulation techniques to character development and performance skills. Participating in these sessions allows you to learn directly from experts, gain practical experience, and receive constructive feedback on your work. In addition to formal workshops, consider seeking out mentorship opportunities. Connecting with a seasoned puppeteer who can guide you through your artistic journey can be transformative. A mentor can provide insights into the industry, share their experiences, and offer personalized advice tailored to your goals. This one-on-one relationship can foster growth and inspire you to push the boundaries of your creativity. Online courses and tutorials have also become increasingly popular, providing accessible learning options for puppeteers around the world. Platforms like Skillshare, Udemy, and YouTube host a plethora of resources covering various aspects of puppetry. Whether you are interested in mastering specific techniques or exploring new styles, these online offerings allow you to learn at your own pace and revisit concepts as needed. Engaging with literature on puppetry can further enrich your understanding of the art form. Books, articles, and academic journals dedicated to puppetry explore its history, theory, and practice. Reading about the experiences of other puppeteers can inspire you and provide valuable insights into the creative process. Consider joining a book club focused on puppetry literature to engage in discussions and share perspectives with fellow enthusiasts. Lastly, attending performances by other puppeteers is an excellent way to learn and be inspired. Observing different styles, techniques, and storytelling approaches can spark new ideas for your own work. Take note of how other artists engage their audiences, develop characters, and utilize puppetry as a means of expression. This observational learning can inform your practice and encourage you to experiment with new concepts.

Chapter 36: The Business of Puppetry

Monetizing Your Skills

In the vibrant world of puppetry, the artistry and creativity that go into character creation can be transformed into a sustainable livelihood. The journey of monetizing your skills begins with recognizing the unique value you bring to the table. Puppetry is not merely a form of entertainment; it is a multifaceted art that can engage audiences of all ages, convey profound messages, and foster connections. To embark on this journey, consider the various avenues available for monetization. One of the most traditional methods is performing live puppet shows. Whether in theaters, schools, or community events, live performances can attract audiences and generate income through ticket sales. Additionally, creating a repertoire of shows that cater to different demographics—children, adults, or specialized audiences—can enhance your marketability. Another avenue is the creation of digital content. In an age where online platforms dominate, puppetry can find a new home on social media, YouTube, or streaming services. By producing engaging videos that showcase your puppets and their stories, you can build a following and monetize through advertisements, sponsorships, or crowdfunding. Workshops and classes also present a lucrative opportunity. Sharing your expertise in puppetry through teaching can not only generate income but also foster a new generation of puppeteers. Consider offering workshops in schools, community centers, or online platforms, where participants can learn the art of puppetry, character creation, and performance techniques. Merchandising is another effective strategy. Creating and selling puppet characters, whether as physical puppets or digital assets, can provide a steady income stream. Collaborating with local artisans or using online platforms to sell your creations can expand your reach and enhance your brand. Finally, consider the potential of licensing your characters for use in various media. This could include books, television shows, or merchandise. By developing a strong brand around your puppet characters, you can create opportunities for partnerships and collaborations that can significantly boost your income.

Funding Projects

Securing funding for puppetry projects can be a daunting task, yet it is essential for bringing your creative visions to life. Various funding sources can be explored, each with its own set of requirements and expectations. Grants are a prominent option for artists seeking financial support. Numerous organizations, both governmental and private, offer grants specifically for the arts, including puppetry. Researching grant opportunities and crafting compelling proposals that articulate your project's vision, audience engagement, and potential impact can increase your chances of securing funding. Crowdfunding has emerged as a popular method for artists to raise funds for their projects. Platforms such as Kickstarter, Indiegogo, and GoFundMe allow you to present your project to a global audience. By sharing your passion and the unique aspects of your puppetry work, you can encourage supporters to contribute financially. Offering rewards, such as exclusive puppet merchandise or behind-the-scenes access, can incentivize contributions. Sponsorships from local businesses or larger corporations can also provide funding. Building relationships with potential sponsors and demonstrating how their support can benefit their brand through community engagement or visibility can lead to fruitful partnerships. Collaborations with other artists or organizations can also be a viable funding strategy. By pooling resources and sharing costs, you can create larger projects that attract more attention and funding opportunities. Lastly, consider hosting fundraising events. Organizing puppet shows, workshops, or community gatherings can not only raise funds but also engage your audience and build a supportive community around your work.

Managing Finances

Once funding is secured, effective financial management becomes crucial to the sustainability of your puppetry endeavors. Establishing a clear budget for each project is the first step. This budget should outline all anticipated expenses, including materials, venue costs, marketing, and personnel. To facilitate financial tracking, consider using accounting software or spreadsheets to monitor income and expenses. This will provide you with a clear picture of your financial health and help you make informed decisions about future projects. It is also essential to set aside a portion of your income for reinvestment into your puppetry business. This could include purchasing new materials, upgrading equipment, or funding marketing efforts. By reinvesting in your craft, you can continue to grow and evolve as an artist. Understanding the tax implications of your puppetry income is vital. Consult with a tax professional to ensure you are compliant with local regulations and to maximize any potential deductions related to your artistic work. Lastly, consider establishing an emergency fund. The world of puppetry can be unpredictable, and having a financial cushion can provide peace of mind and stability during lean periods. By approaching the business side of puppetry with the same creativity and passion that you apply to your art, you can create a sustainable and fulfilling career that allows you to share your unique characters and stories with the world.

Chapter 37: Adapting Characters for Different Mediums

The world of puppetry is a vibrant tapestry woven from diverse threads of creativity, culture, and innovation. As puppeteers, we are tasked with the exhilarating challenge of breathing life into characters that can traverse various mediums, each with its unique demands and opportunities. Whether it be the intimate setting of a stage, the expansive canvas of film and television, or the boundless realm of digital platforms, adapting our puppet characters requires a keen understanding of the nuances that each medium presents. In this chapter, we will explore the intricacies of adapting puppet characters across different platforms, focusing on the essential elements that make a character resonate, regardless of the medium.

Stage, Screen, and Digital Platforms

The stage is where puppetry often finds its most immediate and visceral expression. The live audience, the palpable energy, and the shared experience create a unique atmosphere that can be both exhilarating and daunting. Characters designed for the stage must possess a certain dynamism, as they are not only seen but also felt. The physicality of the puppets, the clarity of their movements, and the expressiveness of their voices must all be heightened to engage the audience effectively. In contrast, the screen—whether it be television or film—offers a different set of challenges and opportunities. Here, the intimacy of the camera allows for subtler expressions and nuances that may not translate as effectively on stage. Characters can be more detailed, their backstories can be explored in depth, and the visual storytelling can be enhanced through the use of special effects and editing techniques. The puppeteer must adapt their performance to suit the lens, often requiring a more nuanced approach to movement and expression. Digital platforms, including online streaming services and social media, have revolutionized the way puppet characters are created and consumed. The immediacy of digital content allows for rapid experimentation and iteration, enabling creators to respond to audience feedback in real-time. Characters can evolve quickly, adapting to trends and viewer preferences while maintaining their core essence. As we delve deeper into each of these mediums, we will uncover the strategies and considerations that puppeteers must embrace to ensure their characters thrive, regardless of the platform.

Understanding the Medium

To adapt a puppet character effectively, one must first understand the medium in which it will be presented. Each medium has its own set of conventions, audience expectations, and technical requirements. For stage performances, the puppeteer must consider the physical space, the audience's sightlines, and the acoustics of the venue. The character's design should facilitate movement that is visible from a distance, and the voice must project to fill the space. The use of exaggerated expressions and gestures can help convey emotions that resonate with the audience, creating a shared experience that is both engaging and memorable. In film and television, the focus shifts to the camera's perspective. Here, the puppeteer must think about how the character will be framed, the angles that will be used, and the pacing of the performance. Close-ups can reveal subtle emotions, while wide shots can showcase the character's physicality in relation to their environment. The integration of visual effects can also enhance the character's presence, allowing for a more immersive experience. Digital platforms introduce yet another layer of complexity. The rapid consumption of content means that characters must be instantly relatable and engaging. Short attention spans require that the character's essence be communicated quickly and effectively. The use of social media can also influence character development, as creators can interact with their audience and receive immediate feedback, allowing for a more collaborative approach to character adaptation.

Character Design Considerations

When adapting characters for different mediums, the design must be flexible enough to accommodate the specific requirements of each platform. This includes not only the visual aspects of the puppet but also its personality, voice, and movement style. For stage puppetry, characters often benefit from bold colors and distinctive shapes that stand out under stage lights. The design should also allow for a range of movement, enabling the puppeteer to convey a wide array of emotions. The character's voice should be loud and clear, with a tone that matches its personality. In film and television, the design can be more intricate, allowing for finer details that can be captured by the camera. The character's backstory can be woven into its design, with visual cues that hint at its history and motivations. The voice can be more nuanced, with subtle inflections that convey depth and complexity. Digital platforms often call for characters that are visually striking and easily recognizable. The design should be adaptable for various formats, whether it be short videos, animated GIFs, or interactive content. The character's personality should shine through quickly, making it easy for viewers to connect with it in a matter of seconds.

Performance Techniques

The performance techniques employed by puppeteers must also adapt to the medium in which the character is presented. On stage, the puppeteer must engage with the audience directly, using larger-than-life movements and vocalizations to draw them in. The energy of the performance should match the atmosphere of the venue, whether it be a small theater or a large auditorium. In film and television, the performance can be more intimate. The puppeteer must consider the camera's perspective, adjusting their movements and expressions to suit the framing. This often requires a more subtle approach, as the camera can capture nuances that may be lost in a live performance. The use of multiple takes allows for refinement, enabling the puppeteer to hone in on the character's essence. Digital platforms require a different approach altogether. The performance must be engaging from the very first moment, capturing the viewer's attention in a crowded digital landscape. The character's personality should be conveyed quickly, often through a combination of visual gags, clever dialogue, and relatable scenarios. The ability to adapt to trends and audience feedback is crucial, as the digital landscape is ever-changing.

Storytelling Across Mediums

At the heart of character adaptation lies storytelling. Each medium offers unique opportunities for narrative exploration, and the puppeteer must adapt their character's story to fit the platform. In stage performances, storytelling is often linear, with a clear beginning, middle, and end. The character's journey unfolds in real-time, allowing the audience to experience the highs and lows alongside the puppet. The use of live music, sound effects, and audience interaction can enhance the storytelling experience, creating a dynamic and immersive environment. Film and television allow for more complex storytelling structures. Flashbacks, montages, and nonlinear narratives can be employed to deepen the character's backstory and motivations. The visual medium enables the use of symbolism and metaphor, enriching the narrative and allowing for a more profound exploration of themes. Digital platforms often favor bite-sized storytelling, where characters must convey their essence in short bursts. This requires a keen understanding of pacing and timing, as well as the ability to create engaging content that resonates with viewers. The character's story can evolve rapidly, adapting to audience feedback and trends, making it a more collaborative and interactive experience.

Collaborative Creation

Adapting characters for different mediums often involves collaboration with other artists and creators. This collaborative spirit can lead to innovative ideas and fresh perspectives that enhance the character's development. In stage productions, puppeteers often work closely with directors, set designers, and costume designers to create a cohesive vision. The character's design, performance, and story must align with the overall production, ensuring that the puppet fits seamlessly into the narrative. In film and television, collaboration extends to writers, cinematographers, and editors. The character's journey is shaped by the script, and the puppeteer's performance must align with the director's vision. The editing process can also influence how the character is perceived, as pacing and timing play a crucial role in storytelling. Digital platforms often encourage collaboration with a broader range of creators, including animators, graphic designers, and social media strategists. The character's presence must be adapted for various formats, requiring input from multiple disciplines to ensure a cohesive and engaging experience.

Conclusion

As we navigate the diverse landscape of puppetry, the ability to adapt characters for different mediums is an invaluable skill. By understanding the unique demands of each platform, embracing collaboration, and honing our storytelling techniques, we can create puppet characters that resonate with audiences across the spectrum. The journey of character adaptation is one of exploration and creativity, inviting us to push the boundaries of our art and connect with audiences in meaningful ways.

Chapter 38: The Role of Puppetry in Activism

Puppetry, an age-old art form, has the unique ability to transcend barriers, evoke emotions, and convey messages that resonate deeply with audiences. In the realm of activism, puppetry emerges as a powerful medium, capable of addressing social issues, sparking conversations, and inspiring change. This chapter delves into the multifaceted role of puppetry in activism, exploring how puppets can be used to create awareness, engage audiences, and deliver powerful messages.

Creating Awareness

At its core, activism is about raising awareness and advocating for change. Puppetry serves as an exceptional tool for this purpose, as it can present complex issues in a manner that is accessible and relatable. The visual nature of puppetry allows for the simplification of intricate topics, making them digestible for audiences of all ages. Puppets can embody various social issues, from environmental concerns to human rights, allowing performers to illustrate these topics in a way that resonates with viewers. For instance, a puppet representing a polar bear can effectively communicate the urgency of climate change, captivating audiences while simultaneously educating them about the plight of endangered species. The use of puppetry in this context not only informs but also evokes empathy, encouraging audiences to reflect on their own roles in the world. Moreover, puppetry can break down the barriers of language and culture. In a diverse society, where individuals may speak different languages or come from various backgrounds, puppets can serve as a universal language. The visual storytelling inherent in puppetry transcends linguistic limitations, allowing messages to be conveyed through actions, expressions, and emotions. This inclusivity is particularly vital in activism, where the goal is to unite individuals around a common cause. In addition to its visual appeal, puppetry can also incorporate humor and satire, making serious topics more approachable. By using comedic elements, puppeteers can engage audiences in a way that encourages them to think critically about the issues at hand. For example, a puppet character that parodies a politician can highlight the absurdities of certain policies, prompting viewers to question the status quo. This blend of humor and activism can create a memorable experience, leaving a lasting impression on the audience. Furthermore, puppetry can be employed in various settings, from street performances to educational workshops. This versatility allows activists to reach diverse audiences, from children in schools to adults at community events. By adapting the content and style of the puppetry to suit different environments, activists can maximize their impact and ensure that their messages are heard.

Engaging Audiences

Engagement is a crucial aspect of activism, as it fosters a sense of community and encourages individuals to take action. Puppetry, with its interactive nature, provides a unique opportunity to engage audiences in meaningful ways. The immediacy of live performances allows for direct interaction between puppeteers and viewers, creating a dynamic atmosphere that encourages participation. One effective method of engagement is through audience participation. Puppeteers can invite audience members to join in the performance, whether by manipulating puppets themselves or by contributing ideas and suggestions. This collaborative approach not only empowers individuals but also fosters a sense of ownership over the message being conveyed. When audiences feel involved, they are more likely to internalize the issues presented and consider their own roles in effecting change. Additionally, puppetry can serve as a catalyst for dialogue. After a performance, puppeteers can facilitate discussions about the themes explored, encouraging audiences to share their thoughts and experiences. This dialogue can lead to a deeper understanding of the issues at hand and inspire individuals to take action in their own communities. By creating a safe space for conversation, puppetry can bridge gaps between different perspectives and foster a sense of solidarity among participants. The visual and emotional impact of puppetry also plays a significant role in audience engagement. Puppets can evoke a wide range of emotions, from joy to sadness, allowing viewers to connect with the characters on a personal level. This emotional connection can be a powerful motivator for action, as individuals are often compelled to respond when they feel a strong emotional resonance with a cause. Moreover, puppetry can be tailored to suit specific demographics, ensuring that the content is relevant and relatable to the intended audience. For example, performances aimed at children can incorporate playful elements and relatable characters, while those targeting adults may delve into more complex themes. By understanding the audience's needs and preferences, puppeteers can create engaging experiences that resonate deeply and inspire action. In the digital age, puppetry can also extend beyond live performances. Social media platforms provide a space for puppeteers to share their work, reach wider audiences, and engage in conversations about important issues. Short videos featuring puppet characters discussing social justice, environmentalism, or mental health can go viral, spreading awareness and inspiring action on a global scale. This adaptability to modern platforms ensures that the messages conveyed through puppetry remain relevant and impactful.

Powerful Messages

The heart of activism lies in its messages, and puppetry has the capacity to deliver these messages with profound impact. Through storytelling, puppets can convey narratives that resonate with audiences, highlighting the struggles and triumphs of individuals and communities. These narratives can serve as a call to action, urging viewers to reflect on their own beliefs and behaviors. Puppetry allows for the exploration of complex social issues in a nuanced manner. For instance, a puppet character representing a marginalized group can share their experiences, shedding light on the challenges they face. This personal storytelling approach humanizes the issues, fostering empathy and understanding among audiences. By presenting these narratives through the lens of puppetry, activists can create a powerful emotional connection that inspires individuals to advocate for change. Moreover, puppetry can amplify the voices of those who are often silenced or overlooked. By giving a platform to marginalized communities, puppeteers can raise awareness about their struggles and advocate for their rights. This representation is crucial in activism, as it ensures that diverse perspectives are heard and valued. Puppetry can serve as a vehicle for social justice, allowing individuals to share their stories and experiences in a way that resonates with others. The use of symbolism in puppetry can also enhance the potency of the messages conveyed. Puppets can embody abstract concepts, such as hope, fear, or resilience, allowing audiences to engage with these ideas on a deeper level. For example, a puppet representing hope can inspire individuals to envision a better future, motivating them to take action toward achieving that vision. This symbolic representation can create a lasting impact, encouraging audiences to reflect on the themes presented long after the performance has ended. Additionally, puppetry can be a means of challenging societal norms and sparking critical conversations. Through satire and parody, puppeteers can address controversial topics, encouraging audiences to question prevailing attitudes and beliefs. This form of activism can be particularly effective in addressing issues such as inequality, discrimination, and environmental degradation. By using humor and creativity, puppetry can provoke thought and inspire individuals to engage with these topics in a meaningful way.

Chapter 39: Character Development Workshops

Character development workshops serve as a vibrant space where creativity flourishes, and the art of puppetry is explored in depth. These workshops provide an invaluable opportunity for participants to delve into the intricacies of character creation, allowing them to breathe life into their puppets through a structured yet flexible framework. The essence of these workshops lies in their ability to foster collaboration, encourage experimentation, and cultivate a supportive environment where ideas can blossom.

Facilitating Workshops

Facilitating a character development workshop requires a blend of enthusiasm, expertise, and empathy. The facilitator acts as a guide, steering participants through the creative process while allowing room for individual expression. It is essential to create an atmosphere that encourages participants to share their thoughts and ideas freely. This can be achieved through icebreakers and group discussions that set a tone of openness and collaboration.

A successful workshop begins with a clear outline of objectives. What do you want participants to take away from the experience? Whether it's mastering the fundamentals of character design or exploring advanced techniques in puppetry, having a defined goal helps to keep the workshop focused and productive.

In addition to setting objectives, it is crucial to tailor the workshop to the participants' skill levels. Beginners may require more foundational exercises, while experienced puppeteers might benefit from advanced character development techniques. Understanding the diverse backgrounds and experiences of participants allows the facilitator to adapt the content accordingly, ensuring that everyone feels included and challenged.

Moreover, the facilitator should encourage a spirit of experimentation. Puppetry is an art form that thrives on innovation, and participants should feel empowered to take risks with their character designs. By fostering an environment where mistakes are seen as opportunities for growth, facilitators can help participants discover their unique artistic voices.

Exercises and Activities

The heart of any character development workshop lies in its exercises and activities. These hands-on experiences are designed to engage participants and stimulate their creativity. Below are some effective exercises that can be incorporated into workshops to enhance character creation skills:

1. Character Brainstorming Sessions

Begin with a brainstorming session where participants can generate ideas for their puppet characters. Encourage them to think about various aspects, such as personality traits, physical attributes, and backstories. This can be done through free writing or mind mapping, allowing participants to explore their thoughts without the constraints of structure.

2. Character Sketching

Once participants have a clear idea of their character, they can move on to sketching. This exercise allows them to visualize their ideas and experiment with different designs. Encourage participants to focus on the physical attributes of their puppets, considering how these features will influence the character's personality and movement.

3. Voice and Movement Exploration

Voice and movement are crucial elements of puppetry. In this exercise, participants can experiment with different vocal qualities and physical movements that align with their character's personality. Encourage them to embody their characters, exploring how they would move and speak in various situations. This not only helps in character development but also enhances the overall performance quality.

4. Backstory Development

Understanding a character's backstory is essential for creating depth. Participants can engage in writing exercises where they develop their character's history, motivations, and relationships. This can be done through prompts that encourage them to think about pivotal moments in their character's life and how these experiences shape their actions and decisions.

5. Group Feedback Sessions

Feedback is a vital component of the creative process. Organizing group feedback sessions allows participants to share their character concepts and receive constructive criticism from their peers. This collaborative approach not only fosters a sense of community but also helps participants refine their ideas and gain new perspectives.

Building Skills

Character development workshops are not just about creating puppets; they are also about building essential skills that participants can carry into their future endeavors. The following skills can be cultivated through engaging activities and thoughtful facilitation:

1. Creative Thinking

Workshops encourage participants to think outside the box and explore unconventional ideas. By engaging in brainstorming sessions and collaborative exercises, participants learn to embrace creativity and develop innovative solutions to character design challenges.

2. Communication Skills

Effective communication is crucial in puppetry, both in terms of character portrayal and collaboration with fellow artists. Workshops provide a platform for participants to practice articulating their ideas, giving and receiving feedback, and collaborating with others. These skills are invaluable in any artistic endeavor.

3. Problem-Solving Abilities

As participants navigate the character creation process, they will inevitably encounter challenges. Workshops encourage them to approach these obstacles with a problem-solving mindset, fostering resilience and adaptability. Learning to overcome creative blocks and refine ideas is a skill that will serve them well in their artistic journeys.

4. Empathy and Understanding

Puppetry is an art form that often explores the human experience. Through character development, participants learn to empathize with their creations, understanding their motivations and emotions. This skill extends beyond puppetry, enhancing participants' ability to connect with others in their personal and professional lives.

5. Technical Skills

Workshops can also provide opportunities for participants to develop technical skills related to puppetry. Whether it's learning about puppet construction, manipulation techniques, or performance skills, these practical experiences equip participants with the tools they need to bring their characters to life.

Chapter 40: The Influence of Literature on Puppetry

Literature has long served as a wellspring of inspiration for puppeteers, providing a rich tapestry of characters, themes, and narratives that can be transformed into the dynamic world of puppetry. The interplay between the written word and the art of puppetry creates a unique synergy, allowing for the exploration of complex ideas and emotions through the medium of performance. This chapter delves into the profound influence of literature on puppetry, examining classic literary works, modern adaptations, and the myriad character inspirations that emerge from the pages of books.

Classic Literature

Classic literature offers a treasure trove of characters and stories that have stood the test of time. These narratives often encapsulate universal themes of love, loss, adventure, and morality, making them ideal candidates for adaptation into puppet performances. The richness of language and depth of character found in classic works provide puppeteers with a robust foundation upon which to build their performances.

The Timeless Appeal of Shakespeare

Shakespeare's plays, with their intricate plots and multifaceted characters, have inspired countless adaptations in various forms of art, including puppetry. The Bard's ability to capture the human experience resonates deeply, allowing puppeteers to explore themes of ambition, jealousy, and love through their characters. For instance, the tragic figure of Macbeth can be reimagined as a puppet, embodying the internal conflict and moral dilemmas that define his character. The use of puppetry can add a layer of visual storytelling, enhancing the emotional weight of Shakespeare's words.

Fairy Tales and Folklore

Fairy tales and folklore are another rich source of inspiration for puppetry. These stories often feature larger-than-life characters, magical elements, and moral lessons, making them perfect for puppet adaptations. The whimsical nature of fairy tales allows for creative interpretations, where puppeteers can infuse their performances with humor and charm. Characters like Little Red Riding Hood or the Big Bad Wolf can be brought to life through puppetry, engaging audiences of all ages and inviting them to explore the moral lessons embedded within these narratives.

Mythology and Epic Tales

Mythological stories from various cultures provide a fascinating backdrop for puppetry. The grand narratives of gods, heroes, and mythical creatures offer a canvas for puppeteers to explore themes of power, sacrifice, and the human condition. For example, the Greek myth of Persephone can be adapted into a puppet show that highlights the duality of life and death, as well as the cyclical nature of seasons. The visual representation of these characters through puppetry can evoke a sense of wonder and awe, drawing audiences into the rich tapestry of mythological storytelling.

Modern Adaptations

As literature continues to evolve, so too does its influence on puppetry. Modern adaptations of literary works provide fresh perspectives and innovative approaches to storytelling. Puppeteers are increasingly drawing from contemporary literature, reimagining beloved characters and narratives for today's audiences.

Young Adult Literature

The rise of young adult literature has introduced a new generation of characters that resonate with both youth and adults. Stories that explore themes of identity, friendship, and resilience can be effectively translated into puppet performances. Characters from popular series, such as "Harry Potter" or "The Hunger Games," can be adapted into puppets, allowing for a unique exploration of their journeys and struggles. The visual nature of puppetry can enhance the emotional connection between the audience and the characters, making the stories more accessible and engaging.

Graphic Novels and Comics

Graphic novels and comics have gained immense popularity in recent years, offering a vibrant and visually dynamic storytelling medium. The colorful characters and imaginative worlds found in these works lend themselves beautifully to puppetry. Puppeteers can bring to life the dynamic action and humor of graphic novels, creating performances that are both visually stunning and narratively compelling. Characters like Spider-Man or the cast of "Scott Pilgrim" can be transformed into puppets, allowing audiences to experience their adventures in a new and exciting way.

Literary Classics Reimagined

Modern adaptations of literary classics also provide fertile ground for puppetry. Works such as "Pride and Prejudice" or "Moby Dick" can be reinterpreted through the lens of puppetry, allowing for a fresh take on familiar stories. Puppeteers can explore the nuances of character relationships and societal themes, creating performances that resonate with contemporary audiences. The juxtaposition of classic literature with the playful nature of puppetry can lead to innovative interpretations that challenge traditional narratives.

Character Inspirations

The characters that populate literature serve as a wellspring of inspiration for puppeteers. From the heroic to the villainous, the complex to the whimsical, literary characters provide a diverse array of personalities that can be brought to life through puppetry.

Archetypes and Their Adaptations

Literature is replete with archetypal characters that embody universal traits and experiences. The hero, the mentor, the trickster, and the villain are just a few examples of archetypes that can be effectively adapted into puppet characters. Puppeteers can draw upon these archetypes to create relatable and engaging performances that resonate with audiences. For instance, the archetypal hero's journey can be depicted through a puppet character who embarks on a quest, facing challenges and growing along the way.

Complex Characters and Emotional Depth

Literature often delves into the complexities of human emotions, providing puppeteers with a rich source of inspiration for character development. Characters who grapple with inner conflicts, moral dilemmas, or emotional struggles can be brought to life through puppetry, allowing for a deeper exploration of their journeys. For example, a puppet representing a character dealing with grief can convey the nuances of loss and healing through movement and expression, creating a powerful connection with the audience.

Iconic Literary Figures

Iconic literary figures, such as Sherlock Holmes, Elizabeth Bennet, or Jay Gatsby, offer a wealth of inspiration for puppet adaptations. These characters have become cultural touchstones, and their stories resonate across generations. Puppeteers can infuse their performances with the essence of these characters, exploring their motivations, relationships, and the societal contexts in which they exist. The visual representation of these figures through puppetry can breathe new life into their narratives, inviting audiences to engage with their stories in a fresh and exciting way.

Chapter 41: The Importance of Feedback

Receiving Critiques

Receiving critiques is an essential part of the creative process, especially in the realm of puppetry where character development is paramount. The act of creating a puppet character is not merely a solitary endeavor; it is an intricate dance between the creator and the audience, and feedback serves as the rhythm that guides this dance. When we open ourselves to the perspectives of others, we invite a wealth of insights that can illuminate aspects of our characters that we may have overlooked. The first step in receiving critiques is to cultivate an open heart and mind. This means approaching feedback not as a personal attack but as a valuable opportunity for growth. It is crucial to remember that critiques are not reflections of our worth as artists but rather reflections of our work. When we detach our self-esteem from our creations, we can engage with feedback more constructively. Engaging with a diverse group of individuals can enrich the feedback process. Seek out fellow puppeteers, theater enthusiasts, educators, and even children, as their perspectives can provide a multifaceted view of your character. Each audience member brings their own experiences and interpretations, which can unveil new dimensions of your puppet character. For instance, a child may resonate with a puppet's playful nature, while an adult might appreciate its underlying wisdom. When receiving critiques, it is beneficial to ask specific questions that guide the feedback process. Instead of simply asking, "What do you think?" consider asking, "How does this character make you feel?" or "What aspects of the character resonate with you?" Such targeted inquiries can elicit more meaningful responses and help you understand how your character is perceived. It is also important to listen actively during feedback sessions. This means not only hearing the words spoken but also observing body language and emotional reactions. Sometimes, the most profound insights come from the unspoken cues that accompany verbal feedback. By being attuned to these nuances, you can gain a deeper understanding of your character's impact on the audience. After receiving critiques, take time to reflect on the feedback. Not every piece of advice will resonate, and that is perfectly acceptable. The key is to discern which critiques align with your vision for the character and which do not. This reflective process can be enhanced by journaling your thoughts or discussing them with a trusted collaborator. Finally, express gratitude to those who provide feedback. A simple "thank you" can go a long way in fostering a supportive creative community. Acknowledging the time and effort others have invested in your work not only strengthens relationships but also encourages ongoing dialogue and collaboration.

Iterating on Characters

The iterative process of character development is akin to sculpting a masterpiece from a block of marble. Each critique, each moment of reflection, serves as a chisel that refines and shapes the character into a more polished version of itself. Iteration is not merely about making changes; it is about deepening the connection between the character and the audience. When embarking on the journey of iteration, it is essential to revisit the core attributes of your character. What are the fundamental traits that define them? How do these traits manifest in their actions, dialogue, and interactions with other characters? By returning to the essence of your character, you can ensure that any changes made during the iteration process remain true to their identity. One effective method for iterating on characters is to create multiple versions of the same character. This could involve altering their appearance, voice, or even their backstory. By experimenting with different iterations, you can explore how these changes affect the character's dynamics within the narrative. For example, a character who is initially portrayed as timid may become more assertive in a different iteration, leading to new conflicts and resolutions within the story. Collaboration can also play a pivotal role in the iteration process. Working with fellow puppeteers or writers can introduce fresh ideas and perspectives that can breathe new life into your character. Engaging in brainstorming sessions or workshops can spark creativity and lead to innovative character developments that you may not have considered on your own. As you iterate on your character, it is crucial to maintain a balance between innovation and consistency. While it is important to embrace change, it is equally vital to ensure that the character's evolution feels organic and believable. Sudden, drastic changes can alienate the audience, so consider how each iteration aligns with the character's established traits and narrative arc. Documentation is another valuable tool in the iteration process. Keeping a character development journal can help you track changes, insights, and feedback over time. This record not only serves as a reference for future iterations but also allows you to reflect on your growth as a creator. Ultimately, the goal of iteration is to create a character that resonates deeply with the audience. This requires a willingness to experiment, to take risks, and to embrace the unknown. Each iteration brings you one step closer to discovering the heart of your character, and with each refinement, you enhance their ability to connect with others.

Growth Mindset

Embracing a growth mindset is fundamental to the art of puppetry and character creation. This mindset fosters resilience, curiosity, and a passion for continuous improvement. When we adopt a growth mindset, we view challenges as opportunities for learning rather than obstacles to success. This perspective is particularly vital in the realm of puppetry, where the nuances of character development can often feel daunting. At the heart of a growth mindset is the belief that abilities and intelligence can be developed through dedication and hard work. This philosophy encourages puppeteers to embrace the learning process, recognizing that mastery is not an endpoint but a journey. Each character created, each performance delivered, contributes to the tapestry of experience that shapes us as artists. One of the key components of a growth mindset is the willingness to take risks. In the context of character creation, this means stepping outside of your comfort zone and exploring new ideas, styles, and techniques. Perhaps you have always created whimsical characters; consider challenging yourself to develop a more serious or complex persona. This willingness to experiment can lead to unexpected breakthroughs and enrich your creative repertoire. Feedback plays a crucial role in cultivating a growth mindset. Rather than viewing critiques as failures, see them as valuable insights that can guide your development. Each piece of feedback is a stepping stone on the path to improvement. By embracing this perspective, you can transform the way you approach your work, viewing challenges as integral to your artistic evolution. Moreover, surrounding yourself with a supportive community can significantly enhance your growth mindset. Engage with fellow puppeteers, attend workshops, and participate in discussions that inspire and motivate you. A vibrant community fosters collaboration and encourages the sharing of ideas, which can ignite your creativity and propel you forward in your artistic journey. It is also essential to practice self-compassion as you navigate the ups and downs of character creation. Acknowledge that mistakes are a natural part of the learning process. Instead of berating yourself for perceived shortcomings, treat yourself with kindness and understanding. This compassionate approach allows you to bounce back from setbacks and continue pursuing your artistic goals with renewed vigor. As you cultivate a growth mindset, remember to celebrate your progress, no matter how small. Each step forward, each character developed, is a testament to your dedication and passion. By recognizing and honoring your achievements, you reinforce the belief that growth is possible and that your efforts are worthwhile.

Chapter 42: Creating a Puppet Character for Social Change

Identifying Issues

In the vibrant tapestry of society, myriad issues demand attention, from environmental concerns to social justice, mental health awareness, and beyond. The art of puppetry, with its unique ability to engage audiences of all ages, serves as a powerful medium for addressing these pressing matters. The first step in creating a puppet character for social change is to identify the issue that resonates deeply with you and your intended audience. Consider the themes that stir your passion. Is it the plight of the environment, the struggles of marginalized communities, or the importance of mental health? Each issue presents an opportunity to craft a character that embodies the essence of the struggle, offering a voice to those who may feel unheard. For example, if you choose to focus on environmental issues, you might create a puppet character that personifies nature itself—a wise old tree or a playful river sprite. This character could navigate the challenges of pollution, deforestation, or climate change, engaging the audience in a dialogue about their role in preserving the planet. Moreover, it is essential to conduct thorough research on the issue at hand. Understanding the nuances of the topic will allow you to create a character that is not only relatable but also informed. This depth of knowledge can transform a simple puppet show into a compelling narrative that educates and inspires action.

Character Messaging

Once you have identified the issue, the next step is to develop a clear and impactful message through your puppet character. The character should serve as a conduit for the themes you wish to explore, embodying the values and emotions associated with the cause. Consider the character's personality traits, motivations, and conflicts. A puppet character addressing mental health might be a quirky, endearing figure who struggles with anxiety but learns to navigate their feelings with the help of friends. This character can resonate with audiences who face similar challenges, fostering a sense of connection and understanding. In crafting your character's messaging, think about the language and tone that will best convey your message. The dialogue should be accessible and engaging, allowing the audience to grasp the complexities of the issue without feeling overwhelmed. Humor can also play a vital role in character messaging, as it can disarm the audience and create a more inviting atmosphere for difficult conversations. Additionally, consider how your character can inspire action. What call to action can you embed within the narrative? Whether it's encouraging viewers to participate in local clean-up efforts or advocating for mental health resources, your puppet character should empower the audience to take tangible steps toward change.

Impactful Storytelling

At the heart of puppetry lies the art of storytelling. To create a puppet character for social change, you must weave a narrative that captivates and resonates with your audience. The story should not only entertain but also provoke thought and inspire empathy. Begin by outlining the character's journey. What challenges do they face? How do they evolve throughout the story? A compelling narrative arc will keep the audience engaged while allowing them to witness the character's growth and transformation. For instance, if your puppet character is an advocate for social justice, their story might involve overcoming obstacles, such as facing discrimination or rallying a community to stand up against injustice. Through their experiences, the audience can gain insight into the struggles faced by marginalized groups, fostering a deeper understanding of the issue. Incorporate elements of conflict and resolution to create a dynamic storytelling experience. The character's struggles should reflect the broader societal issues at play, allowing the audience to draw parallels between the puppet's journey and their own lives. Moreover, consider the use of visual storytelling techniques. The design of the puppet, the setting, and the use of props can all enhance the narrative and reinforce the character's message. A vibrant, colorful puppet can symbolize hope and resilience, while a darker, more subdued character might represent the weight of societal issues. Ultimately, the goal of impactful storytelling in puppetry is to create a space for dialogue and reflection. By inviting the audience to engage with the character's journey, you can foster a sense of community and shared responsibility for the issues at hand.

Case Study: The Eco-Warrior Puppet

In a small town grappling with pollution and environmental degradation, a local puppeteer created an eco-warrior puppet named "Wanda the Wise Willow." Wanda, a charming and animated tree puppet, became a beloved figure in the community. Through her adventures, she educated children about recycling, conservation, and the importance of protecting natural habitats. Wanda's story began with her witnessing the destruction of her forest home due to littering and industrial waste. As she journeyed through the town, she encountered various characters, including a mischievous raccoon who hoarded trash and a group of children who were unaware of their impact on the environment. Through engaging storytelling, Wanda taught the children about the importance of reducing waste and taking care of their surroundings. The puppet shows sparked conversations among families, leading to community clean-up events and a renewed commitment to environmental stewardship. Wanda's character not only entertained but also inspired action, demonstrating the profound impact that a puppet character can have in promoting social change.

Case Study: The Mental Health Advocate

In another instance, a puppeteer created a character named "Benny the Brave Bunny," who struggled with anxiety and self-doubt. Benny's journey resonated with children and adults alike, as he navigated the challenges of mental health in a relatable and humorous way. The puppet shows featured Benny facing everyday situations that triggered his anxiety, such as speaking in front of a crowd or trying new activities. With the help of his friends, Benny learned coping strategies and the importance of seeking support. The character's messaging emphasized that it is okay to feel anxious and that reaching out for help is a sign of strength. Benny's story encouraged open discussions about mental health, reducing stigma and fostering a supportive community. As a result, local schools began incorporating mental health education into their curricula, inspired by Benny's adventures. The puppet character became a symbol of resilience, reminding audiences that they are not alone in their struggles.

Case Study: The Social Justice Puppet

A talented puppeteer in an urban setting created a character named "Justice the Jolly Giraffe," who advocated for social justice and equality. Justice's vibrant personality and catchy songs made her a hit among children, while her messages about inclusivity and standing up against discrimination resonated with audiences of all ages. Justice's story involved her journey through a diverse neighborhood, where she encountered various characters facing discrimination based on race, gender, and ability. Through her interactions, she taught the importance of empathy, understanding, and allyship. The puppet shows sparked conversations in schools and community centers, encouraging audiences to reflect on their own biases and take action against injustice. Justice's character became a catalyst for change, inspiring local initiatives aimed at promoting diversity and inclusion. In creating puppet characters for social change, the possibilities are as boundless as the imagination. By identifying pressing issues, crafting meaningful character messaging, and engaging in impactful storytelling, puppeteers can harness the power of this art form to inspire action and foster a more compassionate world. The journey of creating a puppet character for social change is not merely about entertainment; it is a profound opportunity to ignite conversations, challenge perceptions, and ultimately, make a difference in the lives of others.

Chapter 43: The Intersection of Puppetry and Visual Arts

Puppetry, a time-honored form of storytelling, has long been intertwined with the visual arts, creating a rich tapestry of expression that captivates audiences of all ages. The marriage of these two disciplines allows for a unique exploration of character, emotion, and narrative, where the puppet becomes a canvas for artistic innovation. This chapter delves into the artistic techniques that enhance puppetry, the collaborative efforts between puppeteers and visual artists, and the exciting realm of mixed media that expands the boundaries of traditional puppetry.

Artistic Techniques

At the heart of puppetry lies a myriad of artistic techniques that breathe life into inanimate objects. The manipulation of form, color, and texture plays a pivotal role in character creation, allowing puppeteers to convey complex emotions and narratives through their creations. One of the foundational techniques in puppetry is sculpting. Whether using clay, foam, or other materials, sculpting allows artists to create distinctive facial features and expressions that resonate with audiences. The subtleties of a raised eyebrow or a downturned mouth can communicate a wealth of emotion, making the puppet relatable and engaging. Painting is another essential technique that enhances the visual appeal of puppets. The choice of colors can evoke specific moods or themes, while intricate designs can tell a story in themselves. For instance, a puppet adorned with vibrant colors may represent joy and exuberance, while darker hues might suggest mystery or sadness. The application of paint can also add depth and dimension, transforming a flat surface into a three-dimensional character. Textile arts play a significant role in puppetry as well. The selection of fabrics for costumes can greatly influence a puppet's personality. Soft, flowing materials may suggest grace and elegance, while rough, textured fabrics can imply ruggedness or strength. The layering of fabrics can create visual interest and complexity, inviting the audience to explore the character's backstory through their attire. Additionally, the use of props and set design can elevate the storytelling experience. A well-crafted backdrop can transport the audience to another world, while carefully chosen props can enhance the narrative. For example, a puppet holding a flower may symbolize innocence or love, while a puppet wielding a sword may represent conflict or bravery. The interplay between puppets and their environment is crucial in creating a cohesive and immersive experience. Lighting is another artistic technique that can dramatically alter the perception of a puppet character. The strategic use of light and shadow can create mood and atmosphere, highlighting specific features or actions. A spotlight on a puppet can draw attention to its emotional expression, while dim lighting can evoke a sense of mystery or suspense. Sound design, though often overlooked, is an integral part of the artistic process in puppetry. The choice of music, sound effects, and voice can enhance the emotional depth of a character. A whimsical tune may accompany a lighthearted puppet, while a somber melody can underscore a poignant moment. The synchronization of sound with movement creates a harmonious experience that resonates with the audience. Incorporating these artistic techniques into puppetry not only enriches the character but also deepens the audience's connection to the story being told. The visual and auditory elements work in tandem to create a multi-sensory experience that captivates and engages.

Collaborating with Visual Artists

The collaboration between puppeteers and visual artists is a dynamic and fruitful partnership that can lead to innovative and groundbreaking work. By combining their unique skills and perspectives, these artists can push the boundaries of traditional puppetry and create truly extraordinary performances. Visual artists bring a wealth of creativity and expertise to the table. Their understanding of color theory, composition, and design can greatly enhance the visual impact of a puppet show. By working closely with puppeteers, visual artists can help to develop a cohesive aesthetic that aligns with the narrative and emotional tone of the performance. One of the most exciting aspects of collaboration is the opportunity for cross-pollination of ideas. Puppeteers may have a specific vision for a character, but a visual artist's interpretation can introduce new elements that enrich the character's design. For example, a puppeteer may envision a whimsical creature, but a visual artist might suggest incorporating elements of surrealism or abstraction, resulting in a puppet that is both imaginative and thought-provoking. Moreover, the collaboration can extend beyond character design to include set design and overall production aesthetics. A visual artist can create a captivating backdrop that complements the puppets and enhances the storytelling. The interplay between the puppets and their environment can create a more immersive experience for the audience, drawing them into the world of the performance. Workshops and collaborative projects can serve as a breeding ground for new ideas and techniques. By bringing together puppeteers and visual artists, these environments foster creativity and experimentation. Artists can share their skills and knowledge, learning from one another and discovering new ways to express their artistic visions. In addition to traditional visual artists, puppeteers can also collaborate with digital artists and animators. The integration of technology into puppetry opens up a world of possibilities, allowing for the creation of hybrid performances that blend live puppetry with digital projections or animations. This fusion can create a mesmerizing experience that captivates audiences and challenges their perceptions of what puppetry can be. Ultimately, the collaboration between puppeteers and visual artists is a celebration of creativity and innovation. By working together, these artists can create performances that are not only visually stunning but also emotionally resonant, leaving a lasting impression on their audiences.

Mixed Media

The realm of mixed media in puppetry is an exciting frontier that allows for the exploration of diverse materials and techniques. By incorporating various artistic mediums, puppeteers can create unique and engaging performances that challenge traditional notions of puppetry. Mixed media puppetry often involves the integration of different materials, such as paper, fabric, wood, and found objects. This eclectic approach allows artists to experiment with texture, form, and color, resulting in puppets that are visually striking and conceptually rich. For instance, a puppet made from recycled materials may carry an environmental message, while one crafted from delicate paper may evoke a sense of fragility and transience. The use of technology in mixed media puppetry has also gained popularity in recent years. Digital projections, video mapping, and interactive elements can enhance the storytelling experience, creating a dynamic interplay between the puppet and its environment. For example, a puppet may interact with projected images, responding to changes in the visual landscape and creating a sense of dialogue between the two. Sound design plays a crucial role in mixed media performances as well. The incorporation of live music, soundscapes, and recorded audio can elevate the emotional impact of the performance. By blending different auditory elements, artists can create a rich sound environment that complements the visual aspects of the puppetry. The exploration of mixed media also encourages innovation in character design. Puppeteers can draw inspiration from various artistic movements, such as surrealism, cubism, or abstract expressionism, to create characters that defy conventional forms. This experimentation can lead to the development of puppets that are not only visually captivating but also thought-provoking, inviting audiences to engage with the performance on a deeper level. Moreover, mixed media puppetry often blurs the lines between different art forms, creating a multidisciplinary experience. The integration of dance, theater, visual arts, and music can result in performances that are rich in texture and complexity. This fusion of disciplines allows for a more holistic approach to storytelling, where each element contributes to the overall narrative. The beauty of mixed media puppetry lies in its ability to challenge expectations and invite audiences to see puppetry in a new light. By embracing diverse materials and techniques, artists can create performances that are not only visually stunning but also intellectually stimulating, encouraging viewers to reflect on the themes and messages presented.

Chapter 44: The Role of Puppetry in Cultural Preservation

Traditional Puppetry Forms

Puppetry, as an art form, has a rich tapestry woven from the threads of diverse cultures around the globe. Each tradition carries its own unique characteristics, reflecting the values, beliefs, and histories of the communities from which they originate. Traditional puppetry forms serve not only as entertainment but also as vessels for cultural expression, storytelling, and education. From the intricate shadow puppets of Indonesia to the vibrant marionettes of Italy, each style embodies the spirit of its culture. The Javanese wayang kulit, for instance, utilizes flat leather puppets to narrate tales from the Ramayana and Mahabharata, engaging audiences with both visual artistry and profound moral lessons. The manipulation of light and shadow creates a mesmerizing spectacle that transcends mere performance, inviting viewers into a world where the divine and the earthly coexist. In contrast, the Bunraku puppetry of Japan showcases the delicate craftsmanship of three-dimensional puppets, operated by skilled puppeteers who are often visible to the audience. This form emphasizes the emotional depth of the characters, as the puppeteers' movements breathe life into the puppets, allowing them to express a wide range of human emotions. The intricate costumes and elaborate staging further enhance the storytelling, making each performance a celebration of Japanese culture and artistry. The European tradition of puppetry, particularly in countries like France and Germany, has its own distinct flair. The famous Guignol puppets of Lyon, for example, are characterized by their humorous and satirical portrayal of everyday life, often addressing social issues through comedy. This blend of entertainment and commentary has made Guignol a beloved figure in French culture, demonstrating how puppetry can serve as a mirror to society. In the Americas, indigenous puppetry traditions, such as the Mexican marionettes known as "títeres," reflect the rich heritage of storytelling passed down through generations. These puppets often depict folklore and legends, preserving the cultural narratives that define communities. The vibrant colors and intricate designs of the puppets not only captivate audiences but also serve as a reminder of the importance of cultural identity. The preservation of these traditional forms of puppetry is crucial in a rapidly changing world. As globalization continues to influence cultural practices, there is a risk of losing these unique art forms. Efforts to document, teach, and promote traditional puppetry are essential in ensuring that future generations can appreciate and participate in this rich cultural heritage.

Storytelling Heritage

At the heart of puppetry lies the art of storytelling. Puppets have been used for centuries to convey narratives that resonate with audiences, often reflecting the moral, ethical, and social values of the cultures from which they emerge. This storytelling heritage is not merely a means of entertainment; it serves as a vital tool for cultural transmission, allowing communities to share their histories, beliefs, and traditions. In many cultures, storytelling through puppetry is intertwined with rituals and ceremonies. For instance, in India, the traditional puppetry form known as "Rajasthani Kathputli" is often performed during festivals and religious events. The puppets, crafted from wood and adorned with colorful fabrics, bring to life tales from Hindu mythology, engaging audiences in a shared cultural experience. This connection between puppetry and ritual underscores the significance of storytelling as a means of preserving cultural identity. Moreover, puppetry has the unique ability to address complex social issues in a manner that is accessible and engaging. Through the lens of puppetry, difficult topics such as gender roles, environmental concerns, and social justice can be explored in a way that encourages dialogue and reflection. For example, the use of puppetry in educational settings has proven effective in teaching children about empathy, diversity, and inclusion. By presenting these themes through relatable characters, puppetry fosters understanding and compassion among young audiences. The storytelling heritage of puppetry also extends to the realm of folklore and mythology. Many cultures utilize puppets to narrate ancient tales that have shaped their identities. The use of puppetry to tell these stories not only entertains but also reinforces cultural values and traditions. In this way, puppetry acts as a bridge between the past and the present, ensuring that the wisdom of previous generations is not lost. Furthermore, the adaptability of puppetry allows for the incorporation of contemporary issues into traditional narratives. Puppeteers often draw inspiration from current events, weaving them into their performances to create a dialogue between the past and the present. This dynamic interplay between tradition and innovation enriches the storytelling experience, making it relevant to modern audiences while honoring the roots of the art form. As we explore the role of puppetry in cultural preservation, it becomes evident that storytelling is a powerful vehicle for transmitting knowledge and values. The ability of puppets to embody characters and convey emotions allows for a deeper connection between the audience and the narrative, fostering a sense of community and shared understanding.

Reviving Lost Arts

In an age where technology dominates the landscape of entertainment, the revival of traditional puppetry forms has become increasingly important. Many of these art forms, once vibrant and integral to cultural expression, have faced the threat of extinction due to changing societal values and the allure of modern media. However, there is a growing movement dedicated to reviving these lost arts, ensuring that the magic of puppetry continues to enchant future generations. One of the most effective ways to revive traditional puppetry is through education and community engagement. Workshops, festivals, and performances provide opportunities for individuals to learn about the history and techniques of puppetry. By involving local communities in these initiatives, puppetry becomes a shared experience that fosters pride in cultural heritage. For instance, community-based puppetry projects often encourage participants to create their own puppets and stories, allowing them to explore their cultural identities while honing their artistic skills. Additionally, the integration of traditional puppetry into contemporary art forms has proven to be a successful strategy for revival. Collaborations between puppeteers and artists from various disciplines, such as theater, dance, and visual arts, have resulted in innovative performances that breathe new life into traditional narratives. These interdisciplinary approaches not only attract diverse audiences but also highlight the versatility of puppetry as an art form. The use of digital media has also played a significant role in the revival of puppetry. Online platforms and social media have provided puppeteers with new avenues to showcase their work, reaching audiences far beyond their local communities. Virtual performances, tutorials, and behind-the-scenes content allow for greater accessibility and engagement, inspiring a new generation of puppeteers and enthusiasts. Moreover, the revival of lost arts often involves the documentation and preservation of traditional techniques. Archiving the knowledge of master puppeteers and recording their methods ensures that these skills are not lost to time. Organizations dedicated to the preservation of cultural heritage often collaborate with puppeteers to create resources that can be shared with aspiring artists, fostering a sense of continuity within the art form. As we navigate the complexities of a globalized world, the revival of traditional puppetry forms serves as a reminder of the importance of cultural diversity. By celebrating and preserving these art forms, we honor the unique stories and traditions that shape our collective human experience. The journey of reviving lost arts is not merely about preserving the past; it is about creating a vibrant future where the magic of puppetry continues to inspire, educate, and connect us all.

Chapter 45: Exploring Puppetry Techniques from Around the World

Puppetry, as an art form, transcends borders and cultures, weaving a rich tapestry of techniques and styles that reflect the diverse human experience. From the intricately crafted marionettes of Europe to the vibrant shadow puppets of Asia, each region has contributed its unique flair to the world of puppetry. This chapter delves into the various puppetry techniques employed across the globe, highlighting their distinctive characteristics, cultural significance, and the artistry involved in their creation.

Global Styles

Puppetry is a universal language, spoken in myriad dialects across continents. Each style tells a story, often rooted in the traditions and histories of the people who create them.

Asian Puppetry

In Asia, puppetry has a long and storied history, with forms such as Wayang Kulit from Indonesia, Bunraku from Japan, and Kathakali from India. Wayang Kulit, or shadow puppetry, utilizes intricately carved leather puppets that are illuminated from behind, casting enchanting shadows on a screen. The stories often draw from ancient epics like the Ramayana and Mahabharata, blending mythology with moral lessons. Bunraku, on the other hand, is a traditional Japanese puppet theater that features large, intricately designed puppets operated by multiple puppeteers. Each puppeteer is trained to manipulate a specific part of the puppet, creating a seamless and lifelike performance. The narratives often explore themes of love, betrayal, and the complexities of human relationships, resonating deeply with audiences. Kathakali, a classical dance-drama from Kerala, India, combines elaborate costumes, makeup, and expressive movements to tell stories from Hindu mythology. The puppets in Kathakali are often larger than life, and the performances are rich in symbolism and emotion, captivating audiences with their vibrant colors and dramatic storytelling.

European Puppetry

In Europe, puppetry has evolved into various forms, each reflecting the cultural nuances of its region. The marionette theater, particularly popular in countries like Italy and France, features puppets controlled by strings, allowing for intricate movements and expressions. The famous Italian commedia dell'arte has influenced many puppet characters, giving rise to iconic figures like Punch and Judy in England, who embody the playful and often mischievous spirit of the tradition. The Czech Republic is renowned for its rich puppetry heritage, with the Prague National Marionette Theatre showcasing performances that blend humor, satire, and social commentary. Czech puppetry often incorporates folk tales and legends, bringing to life characters that resonate with both children and adults.

African Puppetry

African puppetry is deeply intertwined with the continent's rich oral traditions and cultural practices. The use of puppets in storytelling serves not only as entertainment but also as a means of preserving history and imparting moral lessons. In countries like Nigeria, traditional puppetry often features brightly colored figures that represent animals or ancestral spirits, conveying messages about community values and social issues. The use of puppetry in rituals and ceremonies is also prevalent in many African cultures. Puppets may be employed to invoke spirits or to celebrate significant life events, such as births, marriages, and funerals. This connection to spirituality and community underscores the importance of puppetry as a cultural expression.

Unique Techniques

The techniques employed in puppetry vary widely, each contributing to the overall aesthetic and emotional impact of the performance.

Manipulation Styles

Puppeteers employ various manipulation styles, each requiring a unique set of skills and techniques. In marionette theater, puppeteers master the art of string manipulation, ensuring that the puppet's movements are fluid and lifelike. This technique demands precision and coordination, as the puppeteer must control multiple strings simultaneously to create a cohesive performance. In contrast, hand puppetry relies on the puppeteer's physical presence and expressiveness. The puppeteer's body language and facial expressions play a crucial role in bringing the puppet to life. This technique fosters a direct connection between the puppeteer and the audience, as the puppeteer often interacts with the audience, breaking the fourth wall and inviting participation. Shadow puppetry, as seen in Wayang Kulit, employs light and shadow to create a mesmerizing visual experience. The puppeteer skillfully manipulates the puppets to cast intricate shadows on a screen, allowing the audience to engage their imagination as they interpret the stories being told. This technique emphasizes the power of suggestion, as the audience fills in the gaps with their creativity.

Material and Craftsmanship

The materials used in puppetry also vary significantly across cultures, influencing the overall aesthetic and durability of the puppets. In many Asian traditions, puppets are crafted from wood, leather, or fabric, each material lending itself to different techniques and styles. The craftsmanship involved in creating these puppets is often passed down through generations, with artisans honing their skills to produce intricate designs that reflect their cultural heritage. In contrast, Western puppetry has embraced a wide range of materials, including foam, plastic, and even digital technology. The advent of modern materials has allowed for greater experimentation and innovation in puppet design, enabling puppeteers to push the boundaries of traditional techniques. This fusion of old and new reflects the evolving nature of puppetry as an art form.

Performance Techniques

Performance techniques in puppetry are as diverse as the styles themselves. Some puppeteers incorporate elements of dance, music, and visual art into their performances, creating a multi-sensory experience for the audience. The integration of live music, for instance, can enhance the emotional depth of a performance, allowing the puppets to resonate with the audience on a deeper level. Improvisation is another technique that many puppeteers employ, allowing for spontaneity and creativity during performances. This approach encourages puppeteers to engage with their audience, responding to their reactions and adapting the performance in real-time. The ability to improvise adds an element of excitement and unpredictability, making each performance a unique experience.

Cultural Significance

Puppetry is not merely a form of entertainment; it serves as a vital cultural expression that reflects the values, beliefs, and histories of communities around the world.

Preservation of Traditions

In many cultures, puppetry plays a crucial role in preserving oral traditions and storytelling practices. The narratives conveyed through puppetry often encapsulate the collective memory of a community, passing down wisdom and cultural heritage from one generation to the next. This preservation of traditions is particularly important in an increasingly globalized world, where unique cultural identities may be at risk of being overshadowed. Puppetry also serves as a medium for social commentary, allowing artists to address contemporary issues and provoke thought within their communities. Through humor and satire, puppeteers can tackle sensitive topics, encouraging dialogue and reflection among audiences. This ability to engage with pressing social issues underscores the relevance of puppetry as a form of artistic expression.

Community Engagement

Puppetry fosters a sense of community, bringing people together through shared experiences. Puppet shows often serve as communal events, where families and friends gather to enjoy performances that resonate with their cultural backgrounds. This communal aspect of puppetry strengthens social bonds and creates a sense of belonging, as audiences connect with the stories and characters presented on stage. In educational settings, puppetry has proven to be an effective tool for engaging children and promoting learning. Through interactive puppet shows, educators can introduce complex concepts in a relatable and entertaining manner, fostering curiosity and creativity among young learners. The use of puppetry in education highlights its versatility as a medium for communication and expression.

Global Exchange

The exchange of puppetry techniques and styles across cultures has enriched the art form, fostering a global appreciation for the diverse expressions of puppetry.

International festivals and workshops provide platforms for puppeteers to share their knowledge and collaborate on projects, creating a vibrant community of artists dedicated to the craft. This global exchange not only enhances the technical skills of puppeteers but also promotes cultural understanding and appreciation. By exploring the puppetry traditions of different cultures, artists can draw inspiration from one another, leading to innovative and hybrid forms of puppetry that reflect the interconnectedness of our world.

Chapter 46: The Future of Puppetry

Emerging Trends

As we stand on the precipice of a new era in puppetry, it is essential to recognize the emerging trends that are shaping the landscape of this timeless art form. The evolution of puppetry is not merely a reflection of technological advancements; it is also a response to the shifting cultural and social paradigms that define our contemporary world. One of the most significant trends is the increasing integration of digital technology into puppetry. Puppeteers are now utilizing augmented reality (AR) and virtual reality (VR) to create immersive experiences that transcend the limitations of traditional puppetry. These technologies allow for the creation of virtual puppets that can interact with audiences in real-time, blurring the lines between the physical and digital realms. This fusion of technology and artistry opens up new avenues for storytelling, enabling puppeteers to craft narratives that are more engaging and interactive than ever before. Moreover, the rise of social media platforms has transformed the way puppeteers connect with their audiences. Puppetry is no longer confined to the stage; it has found a vibrant home online. Creators are leveraging platforms like Instagram, TikTok, and YouTube to showcase their characters and performances, reaching a global audience with unprecedented ease. This democratization of puppetry allows for a diverse range of voices and styles to emerge, enriching the art form and fostering a sense of community among puppeteers and fans alike. In addition to technological advancements, there is a growing emphasis on inclusivity and representation within the puppetry community. Artists are increasingly aware of the importance of reflecting the diverse experiences and identities of their audiences. This shift is leading to the creation of characters that resonate with a broader spectrum of viewers, challenging stereotypes and promoting empathy through storytelling. As puppeteers embrace this responsibility, we can expect to see a richer tapestry of characters that celebrate the uniqueness of human experience.

Innovations in Character Creation

The future of puppetry is not solely defined by technology; it is also characterized by innovative approaches to character creation. Puppeteers are exploring new materials, techniques, and design philosophies that push the boundaries of what a puppet can be. The traditional wooden marionette or cloth puppet is being reimagined through the use of unconventional materials such as recycled plastics, 3D-printed components, and even organic materials like plant fibers. This experimentation not only enhances the visual appeal of puppets but also aligns with a growing consciousness about sustainability in the arts. Furthermore, the process of character development is evolving to include interdisciplinary collaboration. Puppeteers are increasingly partnering with artists from various fields, such as animators, writers, and musicians, to create multifaceted characters that are rich in depth and complexity. This collaborative spirit fosters a dynamic exchange of ideas, resulting in characters that are not only visually striking but also narratively compelling. The blending of different artistic disciplines enriches the storytelling potential of puppetry, allowing for a more holistic approach to character creation. Another noteworthy innovation is the incorporation of interactive elements into puppet performances. Audiences are no longer passive observers; they are invited to engage with the characters in meaningful ways. This interactivity can take many forms, from audience participation in live shows to interactive digital experiences that allow viewers to influence the narrative. By breaking down the barriers between performer and audience, puppeteers are creating a sense of shared experience that enhances the emotional impact of their work.

Predictions

Looking ahead, the future of puppetry is poised for remarkable growth and transformation. As we navigate an increasingly complex world, the role of puppetry as a medium for social commentary and cultural expression will become even more pronounced. Puppeteers will continue to harness their craft to address pressing issues such as climate change, social justice, and mental health, using their characters as vehicles for advocacy and awareness. The ability of puppetry to convey complex emotions and ideas in an accessible manner makes it an invaluable tool for sparking dialogue and inspiring change. Moreover, the continued advancement of technology will undoubtedly influence the evolution of puppetry. We can anticipate the emergence of even more sophisticated tools for puppet manipulation and animation, allowing for greater precision and creativity in performances. As artificial intelligence (AI) becomes more integrated into the creative process, we may witness the development of puppets that can respond to audience emotions in real-time, creating a truly interactive experience that adapts to the mood of the room. In terms of audience engagement, the trend toward personalized experiences will likely gain momentum. As audiences seek more meaningful connections with the art they consume, puppeteers will need to find innovative ways to tailor their performances to individual preferences. This could involve the use of data analytics to understand audience demographics and interests, enabling creators to craft characters and stories that resonate on a personal level. Finally, the global nature of the internet will continue to facilitate cross-cultural exchanges within the puppetry community. Artists from diverse backgrounds will collaborate and share their unique perspectives, leading to the creation of hybrid forms of puppetry that draw from various cultural traditions. This blending of influences will enrich the art form, fostering a greater appreciation for the myriad ways in which puppetry can be expressed and experienced.

Chapter 47: Building a Puppet Character for Children

Child-Friendly Design

Creating puppet characters for children requires a thoughtful approach that prioritizes both aesthetics and functionality. The design of a puppet must resonate with the young audience, capturing their imagination while also being safe and durable. Bright colors, whimsical shapes, and friendly features are essential elements that draw children in. When designing a puppet, consider the age group you are targeting. For toddlers, puppets with oversized heads, large eyes, and simple, exaggerated expressions can be particularly engaging. These features not only attract attention but also help convey emotions clearly, making it easier for young children to connect with the character. As children grow older, they may appreciate more nuanced designs that incorporate elements of storytelling, such as costumes that reflect the character's background or personality. Materials play a crucial role in the design process. Soft fabrics, lightweight materials, and non-toxic paints ensure that the puppet is safe for children to handle. Additionally, the construction should be robust enough to withstand the enthusiastic play of young hands. Consider using a combination of textures to stimulate tactile exploration, such as fuzzy fur for animals or smooth satin for fairy tale characters. The size of the puppet is also important. A puppet that is too large may intimidate younger children, while one that is too small might be difficult for them to manipulate. Striking the right balance ensures that children feel empowered to engage with the puppet, whether they are performing with it or simply enjoying a show. Incorporating interactive elements can enhance the child-friendly design. Puppets that can move their mouths, blink their eyes, or even make sounds can captivate young audiences and encourage participation. This interaction fosters a sense of agency, allowing children to feel as though they are part of the story being told. Ultimately, the goal of child-friendly design is to create puppet characters that are not only visually appealing but also encourage creativity, imagination, and emotional connection. By focusing on these aspects, puppeteers can craft characters that resonate deeply with children, leaving a lasting impression that inspires further exploration of the art of puppetry.

Educational Elements

Puppetry is a powerful tool for education, and when building puppet characters for children, integrating educational elements can enhance the learning experience. These characters can serve as conduits for teaching important concepts, values, and skills in a fun and engaging manner. One effective approach is to create puppet characters that embody specific traits or lessons. For example, a puppet that represents kindness can be used to teach children about empathy and the importance of helping others. Through storytelling and interactive performances, children can learn about social skills, emotional intelligence, and conflict resolution in a relatable context. Incorporating themes from various subjects can also enrich the educational value of puppet shows. Characters can be designed to explore topics such as science, history, or geography. A puppet that embodies a historical figure can bring history to life, making it more accessible and engaging for young learners. For instance, a puppet representing a famous scientist can explain basic scientific concepts in a way that is entertaining and memorable. Language development is another area where puppetry shines. Puppets can be used to introduce new vocabulary, encourage storytelling, and promote communication skills. By engaging children in dialogue with the puppet, they can practice their speaking and listening skills in a low-pressure environment. This interaction can also help build confidence, as children feel more comfortable expressing themselves through a character rather than directly. Moreover, puppetry can foster creativity and critical thinking. By encouraging children to create their own puppet characters and stories, they can explore their imaginations and develop problem-solving skills. Workshops that focus on character creation can empower children to express their ideas and collaborate with peers, enhancing their social skills and teamwork abilities. Incorporating educational elements into puppet characters not only enriches the learning experience but also makes it enjoyable. The combination of entertainment and education creates a dynamic environment where children can thrive, making puppetry a valuable tool in both formal and informal educational settings.

Engaging Narratives

At the heart of any successful puppet character lies a compelling narrative that captivates the audience's attention. Engaging narratives are essential for creating a connection between the puppet and the children, allowing them to invest emotionally in the story being told. When crafting narratives for puppet characters, it is important to consider the interests and experiences of the target audience. Children are naturally curious and imaginative, so stories that spark their interest and encourage them to think critically are particularly effective. Themes of adventure, friendship, and discovery resonate well with young audiences, providing a foundation for engaging storytelling. A well-structured narrative often includes relatable challenges or conflicts that the puppet character must navigate. These challenges can serve as opportunities for children to learn valuable lessons about perseverance, teamwork, and problem-solving. For example, a puppet character who faces obstacles on a quest can inspire children to think creatively about how to overcome difficulties in their own lives. In addition to conflict, humor is a powerful tool in engaging narratives. Children respond positively to humor, and incorporating funny situations or witty dialogue can keep their attention and make the story more enjoyable. A puppet character with a quirky personality or a knack for silly antics can elicit laughter and create a joyful atmosphere, enhancing the overall experience. Interactive storytelling can further enhance engagement. Encouraging children to participate in the narrative—whether through responding to questions, making choices for the puppet, or even joining in on songs and dances—creates a sense of ownership and investment in the story. This interaction not only makes the experience more memorable but also fosters a deeper connection between the children and the puppet character. Ultimately, the goal of engaging narratives is to create a rich tapestry of experiences that resonate with children. By weaving together relatable themes, humor, and opportunities for interaction, puppeteers can craft stories that not only entertain but also inspire and educate young audiences. Through the art of storytelling, puppet characters can become beloved companions on a journey of imagination and discovery.

Chapter 48: The Role of Puppetry in Festivals and Events

Creating Event Characters

Creating characters for festivals and events is an exhilarating endeavor that requires a blend of creativity, cultural awareness, and an understanding of the event's theme. The characters you design must resonate with the audience, embodying the spirit of the occasion while also being visually captivating.

When embarking on this journey, consider the following elements:

1. Theme Alignment

Every festival or event has a unique theme or purpose that guides its atmosphere and activities. Whether it's a cultural celebration, a seasonal festival, or a community gathering, your puppet characters should reflect this theme. For instance, during a harvest festival, characters could be inspired by nature, embodying elements like the sun, moon, or various crops.

2. Cultural Representation

Puppetry has a rich history across various cultures, and incorporating elements from these traditions can enhance the authenticity of your characters. Research local folklore, myths, and legends to create characters that resonate with the community. This not only enriches the performance but also fosters a sense of pride and connection among the audience.

3. Visual Appeal

The visual design of your puppets is crucial in capturing the attention of festival-goers.

Bright colors, intricate patterns, and unique shapes can make your characters stand out in a crowded environment. Consider using materials that reflect the theme of the event, such as biodegradable materials for an eco-friendly festival or shimmering fabrics for a night-time event.

4. Interactive Elements

Incorporating interactive elements into your puppet characters can significantly enhance audience engagement. Think about how your puppets can interact with festival-goers—perhaps they can hand out small tokens, pose for photos, or even lead a dance. This interaction creates memorable experiences that resonate long after the event concludes.

Engaging Audiences

Engaging an audience during a festival or event is an art form in itself. The dynamic nature of festivals means that attention spans can be fleeting, making it essential to capture and hold the audience's interest. Here are some strategies to ensure your puppetry captivates attendees:

1. Storytelling Techniques

Storytelling is at the heart of puppetry. Craft a narrative that is easy to follow yet rich in detail. Use your characters to tell a story that aligns with the festival's theme. For example, if you are performing at a cultural festival, consider weaving in traditional tales or legends that highlight the significance of the event.

2. Use of Humor

Humor is a universal language that can break down barriers and create a joyful atmosphere. Incorporate comedic elements into your performances, whether through witty dialogue, physical comedy, or playful interactions with the audience. A well-timed joke or a humorous mishap can elicit laughter and create a bond between the puppets and the audience.

3. Dynamic Performances

The energy of your performance should match the vibrancy of the festival. Use varied pacing, dramatic pauses, and lively movements to keep the audience engaged. Consider incorporating music and sound effects to enhance the performance, creating an immersive experience that draws the audience in.

4. Audience Participation

Encouraging audience participation can transform a passive viewing experience into an interactive celebration. Invite attendees to join in on the fun—whether it's through singing, dancing, or even helping to control a puppet. This not only makes the performance more enjoyable but also fosters a sense of community among festival-goers.

5. Social Media Engagement

In today's digital age, leveraging social media can amplify your reach and engagement. Create shareable moments during your performance that encourage attendees to capture and share their experiences online. Consider setting up a photo booth with your puppets or creating a unique hashtag for the event to encourage social media interaction.

Performance Tips

To ensure your puppetry shines during festivals and events, consider the following performance tips:

1. Rehearsal and Preparation

Thorough rehearsal is essential for a polished performance. Practice not only the movements and dialogue of your puppets but also the timing of interactions with the audience. Familiarize yourself with the event space to anticipate any challenges that may arise during the performance.

2. Adaptability

Festivals can be unpredictable, with changes in weather, audience size, and energy levels. Be prepared to adapt your performance to suit the circumstances. If it starts to rain, consider a more intimate performance under a tent, or if the audience is particularly lively, ramp up the energy to match their enthusiasm.

3. Safety Considerations

Safety should always be a priority during performances. Ensure that your puppets are constructed securely and that any props used are safe for both the performers and the audience. Be mindful of the space around you, avoiding hazards that could lead to accidents.

4. Feedback and Reflection

After each performance, take time to reflect on what worked well and what could be improved. Gathering feedback from fellow performers and audience members can provide valuable insights that enhance future performances. Consider keeping a journal to document your experiences and ideas for character development.

5. Networking Opportunities

Festivals and events are excellent opportunities to connect with other artists and performers. Engage with fellow puppeteers, share experiences, and exchange ideas. Building relationships within the puppetry community can lead to collaborations and new opportunities for growth.

6. Enjoy the Moment

Finally, remember to enjoy the experience. Festivals are celebrations of creativity and community, and your enthusiasm will resonate with the audience. Embrace the joy of performing and the connections you make with festival-goers, allowing that energy to enhance your puppetry.

This text provides a comprehensive exploration of the role of puppetry in festivals and events, focusing on character creation, audience engagement, and performance tips. Each section is designed to inspire and inform, ensuring that the reader is equipped with the knowledge to create memorable puppet experiences.

Chapter 49: The Influence of Technology on Character Creation

The world of puppetry has always been a vibrant tapestry woven from threads of creativity, artistry, and innovation. As we stand on the precipice of a new era, the influence of technology on character creation in puppetry cannot be overstated. The advent of digital tools, animation software, and virtual puppetry has opened up a realm of possibilities that were once confined to the imagination. This chapter will explore how these technological advancements have transformed the landscape of puppetry, allowing artists to breathe life into their characters in ways previously unimagined.

Digital Tools

The digital age has ushered in an array of tools that have revolutionized the way puppeteers conceptualize and create their characters. From graphic design software to 3D modeling applications, these digital tools have become indispensable in the modern puppeteer's toolkit. One of the most significant advantages of digital tools is the ability to visualize characters before they are physically constructed. Software such as Adobe Illustrator and Photoshop allows artists to sketch and refine their designs with precision. The layering capabilities of these programs enable puppeteers to experiment with colors, textures, and shapes, ensuring that every aspect of their character is meticulously crafted. This process not only enhances the aesthetic appeal of the puppet but also aids in the development of its personality and backstory. Moreover, digital tools facilitate collaboration among artists. In a world where puppetry often intersects with other art forms, the ability to share and edit designs in real-time fosters a spirit of cooperation and creativity. For instance, a puppeteer can work alongside a costume designer to create a character that is visually cohesive and narratively compelling. This collaborative approach enriches the character creation process, allowing for a more holistic understanding of the puppet's role within a performance. The rise of social media platforms has also played a pivotal role in the dissemination of ideas and inspiration. Artists can showcase their work, receive feedback, and connect with a global community of puppeteers. This exchange of ideas not only fuels individual creativity but also contributes to the evolution of puppetry as a whole. As artists share their digital creations, they inspire others to push the boundaries of what is possible, leading to a vibrant and ever-evolving art form.

Case Study: The Digital Puppet Revolution

Consider the case of a contemporary puppeteer who embraced digital tools to create a character for a modern puppet show. Utilizing software like Blender, they designed a 3D puppet that could be manipulated in real-time during performances. This innovative approach allowed for a level of expressiveness and fluidity that traditional puppetry often struggles to achieve. The puppeteer began by sketching their character digitally, experimenting with various designs until they found the perfect balance of whimsy and depth. Once the design was finalized, they used Blender to create a 3D model, complete with rigging that allowed for intricate movements. This digital puppet could be animated and controlled via a tablet, enabling the puppeteer to perform with a level of precision that captivated audiences. The success of this digital puppet not only showcased the potential of technology in character creation but also inspired other artists to explore similar avenues. The fusion of traditional puppetry with digital tools opened up new possibilities for storytelling, allowing for a richer and more immersive experience for audiences.

Animation Software

Animation software has become a cornerstone of modern puppetry, providing artists with the means to bring their characters to life in dynamic and engaging ways. Programs such as Toon Boom Harmony and Adobe Animate allow puppeteers to create animated sequences that can complement live performances or stand alone as digital works of art. The integration of animation into puppetry offers a unique opportunity for character development. Through animation, puppeteers can explore the nuances of their characters' personalities, showcasing their emotions and reactions in ways that may not be possible in a traditional puppet show. This added layer of depth enriches the storytelling experience, allowing audiences to connect with characters on a more profound level. Furthermore, animation software enables the creation of hybrid performances that blend live puppetry with animated elements. This innovative approach allows for a seamless integration of digital and physical puppetry, creating a captivating visual experience. For instance, a puppeteer might perform with a physical puppet while simultaneously animating a digital counterpart, enhancing the narrative and expanding the possibilities of character interaction. The accessibility of animation software has also democratized the art of puppetry. Aspiring puppeteers can experiment with character creation and animation without the need for extensive resources or training. Online tutorials and communities provide valuable support, empowering individuals to explore their creativity and develop their skills.

Case Study: Animated Puppetry in Education

A notable example of animation software's impact on character creation can be seen in educational settings. A group of educators utilized animation software to create a series of animated puppetry videos aimed at teaching children about environmental conservation. By designing vibrant, relatable characters, they were able to engage young audiences and convey important messages in an entertaining manner. The educators began by brainstorming character concepts that would resonate with children. They used animation software to bring these characters to life, creating short animated clips that featured the puppets discussing environmental issues in a fun and accessible way. The combination of lively animation and relatable characters captured the attention of students, making learning an enjoyable experience. This project not only demonstrated the power of animation in character creation but also highlighted the potential of puppetry as an educational tool. By leveraging technology, the educators were able to create a lasting impact on their students, fostering a sense of responsibility and awareness about environmental issues.

Virtual Puppetry

As technology continues to advance, virtual puppetry has emerged as a groundbreaking frontier in the world of character creation. Utilizing virtual reality (VR) and augmented reality (AR), puppeteers can create immersive experiences that transport audiences into fantastical worlds where their characters come to life in unprecedented ways. Virtual puppetry allows for a level of interactivity that traditional puppetry cannot achieve. Audiences can engage with characters in real-time, influencing their actions and decisions through their interactions. This dynamic relationship between the audience and the puppet creates a sense of agency, making the experience more personal and memorable. The use of VR technology in puppetry has opened up new avenues for storytelling. Puppeteers can design entire virtual environments where their characters can roam freely, interact with other characters, and embark on adventures. This immersive approach not only enhances the narrative but also invites audiences to become active participants in the story. Moreover, virtual puppetry has the potential to reach audiences far beyond the confines of a physical stage. With the ability to stream performances online, puppeteers can share their work with a global audience, breaking down geographical barriers and expanding their reach. This accessibility allows for a diverse range of voices and stories to be heard, enriching the art form as a whole.

Case Study: Virtual Reality Puppet Theatre

A pioneering example of virtual puppetry can be found in a project that utilized VR technology to create an interactive puppet theater experience. The creators designed a virtual environment where audiences could don VR headsets and step into a whimsical world populated by charming puppet characters. In this virtual theater, audiences could interact with the puppets, influencing their actions and decisions. For instance, a character might ask for help solving a puzzle, and audience members could collaborate to find the solution. This level of interactivity transformed the traditional passive viewing experience into an engaging and participatory adventure. The success of this virtual puppet theater not only showcased the potential of technology in character creation but also highlighted the importance of audience engagement in storytelling. By inviting viewers to become active participants, the creators fostered a deeper connection between the audience and the characters, resulting in a memorable and impactful experience. As we navigate the ever-evolving landscape of puppetry, it is clear that technology will continue to play a pivotal role in character creation. Digital tools, animation software, and virtual puppetry have expanded the horizons of what is possible, allowing artists to explore new dimensions of creativity and storytelling. The fusion of traditional puppetry with modern technology not only enriches the art form but also invites audiences to engage with characters in ways that resonate deeply within their hearts and minds. The future of puppetry is bright, and the possibilities are as limitless as the imagination itself.

Chapter 50: The Art of Character Transformation

Character Growth

Character transformation is a profound journey that transcends mere physicality, delving deep into the essence of what it means to evolve. In the realm of puppetry, this growth is not only a reflection of the character's experiences but also a mirror to the audience's own journey. Each puppet, regardless of its form, embodies a narrative that resonates with the human experience. The process of character growth begins with the foundation of personality traits and motivations. A puppet, much like a human, must possess desires, fears, and aspirations that drive its actions. As the story unfolds, these elements must be challenged and reshaped. For instance, a once timid puppet may find courage through a series of trials, transforming into a beacon of bravery. This arc not only captivates the audience but also fosters a connection that allows viewers to reflect on their own growth. To effectively portray this transformation, puppeteers must engage in a deep understanding of their characters. This involves exploring the backstory, which serves as the groundwork for growth. A puppet's past experiences shape its present behavior and future decisions. By crafting a rich history, puppeteers can create a believable trajectory of change. For example, a puppet that has faced adversity may develop resilience, while one that has lived a sheltered life may learn the value of empathy through exposure to diverse experiences. Moreover, the emotional depth of a character plays a crucial role in its growth. Audiences are drawn to characters that evoke genuine feelings. A puppet that undergoes transformation must navigate a spectrum of emotions, from joy to sorrow, fear to hope. This emotional journey not only enriches the character but also allows the audience to engage on a deeper level. The puppeteer's ability to convey these emotions through movement, voice, and expression is paramount. In addition, the relationships a puppet forms with other characters can significantly influence its growth. Interactions serve as catalysts for change, pushing the puppet to confront its limitations and expand its horizons. For instance, a puppet that initially embodies selfishness may learn the importance of collaboration through friendships forged in adversity. These dynamics create a tapestry of interconnected stories, enriching the overall narrative and providing a fertile ground for character development. Ultimately, character growth in puppetry is a celebration of transformation. It invites audiences to witness the evolution of a character, mirroring their own life experiences. This journey of change, marked by trials and triumphs, resonates deeply, reminding us that growth is a universal experience.

Physical Changes

The physical transformation of a puppet is a captivating aspect of character evolution that can enhance storytelling in profound ways. Just as humans undergo changes throughout their lives, puppets too can reflect these shifts through their appearance, design, and movement. The visual representation of a character's growth is a powerful tool that can communicate emotions and experiences without the need for words. Physical changes can manifest in various forms, from alterations in size and shape to modifications in color and texture. For instance, a puppet that begins its journey as a small, fragile figure may grow larger and more robust as it gains confidence and strength. This transformation can be visually represented through the use of materials that convey resilience, such as sturdier fabrics or more rigid structures. The audience can witness this metamorphosis, which serves as a visual metaphor for the character's internal journey. Moreover, the use of costume design plays a pivotal role in physical transformation. Costumes can signify changes in status, personality, or emotional state. A puppet that starts with drab, muted colors may don vibrant hues as it embraces its newfound identity. Accessories, such as hats or jewelry, can also symbolize milestones in the character's journey. For example, a puppet that has achieved a significant goal might wear a crown or medal, visually marking its accomplishments. Movement is another critical aspect of physical transformation. As a character evolves, its mannerisms and movements can shift dramatically. A puppet that initially moves hesitantly may develop a more confident gait as it gains self-assurance. This change can be achieved through the puppeteer's manipulation, emphasizing the character's growth through fluidity and grace. The contrast between the puppet's initial awkwardness and its eventual poise can create a powerful visual narrative that resonates with the audience. Additionally, the physical transformation of a puppet can be used to symbolize broader themes within the story. For instance, a puppet that undergoes a dramatic change in appearance may reflect societal issues, such as the impact of war, poverty, or personal struggle. By embodying these themes, the puppet becomes a vessel for deeper conversations, inviting audiences to engage with complex topics through the lens of character transformation. The artistry of physical changes in puppetry lies in the ability to weave together visual elements with narrative depth. Each alteration, whether subtle or dramatic, contributes to the overall story, enhancing the audience's understanding of the character's journey. The interplay between physicality and narrative creates a rich tapestry of transformation that captivates and inspires.

Narrative Evolution

The evolution of a character's narrative is a dynamic process that intertwines with both character growth and physical changes. As puppets navigate their stories, the narrative itself must adapt and evolve, reflecting the complexities of life and the intricacies of human experience. This evolution is not merely a linear progression; it is a multifaceted journey that encompasses challenges, revelations, and transformations. At the heart of narrative evolution lies the concept of conflict. Every compelling story requires tension, whether internal or external, that propels the character forward. For puppets, these conflicts can arise from various sources: personal dilemmas, societal pressures, or relationships with other characters. The resolution of these conflicts often leads to significant character transformation, as the puppet learns valuable lessons and gains new perspectives. For example, a puppet facing a moral dilemma may grapple with its values, ultimately leading to a profound shift in its understanding of right and wrong. This internal struggle not only enriches the character but also invites the audience to reflect on their own beliefs and choices. The narrative evolution becomes a shared experience, fostering empathy and connection between the puppet and its viewers. Moreover, the pacing of the narrative is crucial in shaping character transformation. A well-crafted story allows for moments of reflection and growth, interspersed with action and conflict. This ebb and flow creates a rhythm that mirrors the complexities of life. Puppeteers must carefully consider how to balance these elements, ensuring that the character's transformation feels organic and authentic. As the narrative unfolds, the relationships between characters also evolve, influencing the trajectory of transformation. Interactions can serve as pivotal moments that challenge the puppet's beliefs and push it toward growth. A mentor figure, for instance, may guide the puppet through its struggles, imparting wisdom that catalyzes change. Conversely, a rival may force the puppet to confront its weaknesses, igniting a journey of self-discovery. Additionally, the setting plays a vital role in narrative evolution. The world in which the puppet exists can shape its experiences and, consequently, its transformation. A puppet navigating a vibrant, bustling city may encounter diverse characters and situations that broaden its horizons, while one in a secluded village may face more introspective challenges. The environment becomes a character in its own right, influencing the narrative and the puppet's growth. Ultimately, the art of character transformation in puppetry is a harmonious blend of growth, physical changes, and narrative evolution. Each element interconnects to create a rich tapestry of storytelling that resonates with audiences on multiple levels. Through the lens of puppetry, we are reminded of the beauty of transformation, the power of storytelling, and the universal journey of growth that binds us all.

Chapter 51: Celebrating Iconic Puppet Characters

Puppetry, as an art form, has given rise to a plethora of iconic characters that have transcended generations and cultures. These characters, often imbued with unique personalities and compelling narratives, have not only entertained audiences but have also served as cultural touchstones. In this chapter, we will explore some of the most celebrated puppet characters, examining their origins, their impact on culture, and the lessons we can glean from their enduring popularity.

Case Studies

To appreciate the significance of iconic puppet characters, we can delve into a few case studies that exemplify their charm and influence.

The Muppets

The Muppets, created by Jim Henson, are perhaps the most recognizable puppets in the world. Characters like Kermit the Frog, Miss Piggy, and Fozzie Bear have become synonymous with creativity and humor. Kermit, with his signature catchphrase, "Hi-ho, Kermit the Frog here!" embodies a sense of optimism and resilience that resonates with audiences of all ages. Miss Piggy, on the other hand, represents a powerful female archetype, combining glamour with assertiveness. Her catchphrase, "Hiya, Kermie!" is delivered with a blend of affection and authority, making her a beloved figure in the realm of puppetry. The Muppets have not only entertained but have also addressed social issues, such as diversity and acceptance, through their narratives.

Sesame Street

Another iconic puppet ensemble is found in "Sesame Street." Characters like Big Bird, Elmo, and Cookie Monster have become educational icons, teaching children about numbers, letters, and social skills. Big Bird, with his childlike innocence, serves as a gentle guide for young viewers, while Elmo's infectious enthusiasm encourages curiosity and exploration. The show's innovative approach to education through puppetry has made it a staple in households worldwide. The characters' relatability and the show's commitment to inclusivity have contributed to its lasting legacy, making "Sesame Street" a beloved institution in children's programming.

Pinocchio

The tale of Pinocchio, originally a literary character created by Carlo Collodi, has been adapted into various puppet forms, most notably by Disney. The wooden puppet who dreams of becoming a real boy has captured the imagination of audiences for over a century. Pinocchio's journey of self-discovery and moral growth resonates deeply, as he learns the importance of honesty and integrity. The character's transformation from a puppet to a real boy symbolizes the universal quest for identity and acceptance. Pinocchio's story has been retold in numerous adaptations, each adding layers to his character while maintaining the core themes of growth and redemption.

Spitting Image

In the realm of political satire, "Spitting Image" stands out as a groundbreaking puppet show that used caricatured puppets of public figures to comment on current events. The show, which originated in the UK, featured exaggerated representations of politicians and celebrities, providing a humorous yet critical lens on societal issues. Characters like Margaret Thatcher and Ronald Reagan were brought to life with a blend of wit and absurdity, allowing audiences to engage with political discourse in a more accessible manner. The show's impact on political satire has been profound, demonstrating how puppetry can serve as a powerful tool for social commentary.

Impact on Culture

The influence of iconic puppet characters extends far beyond entertainment; they have shaped cultural narratives and societal norms in significant ways.

Representation and Diversity

Puppetry has the unique ability to transcend barriers, allowing for representation of diverse cultures and experiences. Characters like Elmo and Big Bird from "Sesame Street" have played pivotal roles in promoting inclusivity, teaching children about empathy and understanding. Moreover, the Muppets have introduced audiences to a variety of cultural perspectives, showcasing the importance of acceptance and friendship across differences. The ability of puppets to embody various identities fosters a sense of belonging and connection among viewers, reinforcing the idea that everyone has a place in the world.

Social Commentary

Puppet characters often serve as conduits for social commentary, addressing pressing issues in a manner that is both engaging and thought-provoking. Shows like "Spitting Image" have utilized puppetry to critique political figures and policies, encouraging audiences to reflect on the state of their societies. Through humor and satire, these characters challenge the status quo, prompting discussions about power, ethics, and accountability. The ability of puppets to tackle complex topics in an accessible way makes them invaluable tools for fostering dialogue and awareness.

Emotional Connection

The emotional depth of puppet characters allows them to forge strong connections with audiences. Characters like Kermit the Frog and Miss Piggy evoke feelings of nostalgia and affection, reminding viewers of their own experiences and struggles. The relatability of these characters, combined with their unique personalities, creates a bond that transcends age and background. This emotional resonance is a testament to the power of puppetry in storytelling, as it allows for the exploration of universal themes such as love, friendship, and self-discovery.

Lessons Learned

As we celebrate iconic puppet characters, it is essential to reflect on the lessons they impart, both to creators and audiences alike.

The Power of Storytelling

At the heart of every iconic puppet character lies a compelling story. The ability to weave narratives that resonate with audiences is a fundamental aspect of character creation. Whether it is Kermit's journey of self-acceptance or Pinocchio's quest for honesty, these stories remind us of the importance of authenticity and growth. Creators can draw inspiration from these narratives, understanding that well-developed characters with relatable arcs can leave a lasting impact on audiences. The art of storytelling, when combined with the visual and emotional appeal of puppetry, creates a powerful medium for expression.

Embracing Diversity

The celebration of iconic puppet characters highlights the importance of diversity in character creation. By embracing a wide range of identities, backgrounds, and experiences, creators can craft characters that resonate with a broader audience. The success of characters like Elmo and Miss Piggy demonstrates that representation matters. When audiences see themselves reflected in the characters they love, it fosters a sense of belonging and validation. This lesson is vital for aspiring puppeteers and storytellers, encouraging them to create inclusive narratives that celebrate the richness of human experience.

Humor as a Tool for Connection

Humor is a powerful tool in puppetry, allowing characters to engage audiences in a lighthearted yet meaningful way. The Muppets, with their witty banter and comedic timing, exemplify how humor can bridge gaps and foster connections. Incorporating humor into character development not only entertains but also encourages audiences to reflect on deeper themes. The ability to laugh at ourselves and our circumstances can be a transformative experience, reminding us of our shared humanity.

The Importance of Collaboration

The creation of iconic puppet characters often involves collaboration among various artists, writers, and performers. The synergy of different talents can lead to the development of rich, multifaceted characters that resonate with audiences. Aspiring puppeteers should embrace collaboration, recognizing that diverse perspectives can enhance their creative process. By working with others, they can explore new ideas and techniques, ultimately enriching their character development and storytelling. In celebrating these iconic puppet characters, we honor the artistry and creativity that have shaped the world of puppetry. Their stories, impact, and the lessons they impart continue to inspire new generations of puppeteers and audiences alike, ensuring that the art of puppetry remains a vibrant and essential part of our cultural landscape.

Printed in Great Britain
by Amazon